HARBOR FOR OUR HOPE

T0294100

HARBOR FOR OUR HOPE

On Acquiring Peace Amidst Suffering

BY BISHOP IGNATIUS (BRIANCHANINOV)

Translated from the Russian by Elena Borowski
Edited by Holy Trinity Monastery

HOLY TRINITY PUBLICATIONS
The Printshop of St Job of Pochaev
Holy Trinity Monastery
Jordanville, New York
2020

Printed with the blessing of His Eminence,
Metropolitan Hilarion First Hierarch
of the Russian Orthodox Church Outside of Russia

PRINTSHOP OF
SAINT JOB OF POCHAEV

An imprint of

HOLY TRINITY PUBLICATIONS
Holy Trinity Monastery
Jordanville, New York 13361-0036
www.holytrinitypublications.com

ISBN: 978–0–88465–422–3 (paperback)
ISBN: 978–0–88465–439–1 (ePub)
ISBN: 978–0–88465–440–7 (Mobipocket)

Library of Congress Control Number: 2020930848

Cover Image: Vector illustration of Lighthouse on Sunset
by Alexander Smulskiy, ID: 47906380, under license from Shutterstock.com.

Contents

Preface

In 2011 my husband Vladimir's many years of struggle with heart disease reached a new, more trying stage. It became clear that his body, damaged from years of heart insufficiency, was declining. Out of love for my husband and concern that, as his caretaker, I be prepared to give him more than physical support, I began searching for spiritual consolation and found it in the writings of St Ignatius (Brianchaninov) (1807–1867).

St Ignatius struggled most of his adult life with chronic illness and debility. I discovered a depth and breadth of spiritual treasures in the saint's writings, especially in the letters that breathe with intimacy and warmth. Sometimes the letters sounded as if they were addressed directly to us. During the next three and a half years my husband's health continued to decline. What St Ignatius had to say regarding the human condition and how to deal with it gave me comfort and strength. I believe the consolation I derived communicated itself to my husband, who struggled courageously with his declining health without complaint until he peacefully reposed in the Lord in June of 2014.

I also wished to share this writing with my family and friends, but an English translation was not available. That led to negotiations with Holy Trinity Publications, who asked me to focus on two topics: the love of God and human suffering. That is how the letters of this edition were chosen.

From the moment his first work was published in the 1860s, St Ignatius's writing was recognized as authoritative spiritual guidance by major figures of the Russian Orthodox Church such as the Optina elders and others. He speaks on topics developed from close acquaintance with patristic writing; this is material not commonly offered in classroom theology, says Dr Alexei Osipov of the Moscow Theological Academy (2007). St Ignatius's frame of reference was broader than the average reader of his day: he knew Holy Scriptures thoroughly, being able to quote from the Bible and writings of the Holy Fathers, many of whose writings he translated from their original Greek or Latin. St Ignatius's knowledge of several languages (Russian, French, old Greek, Latin, and German) gives his writings exceptional ease of comprehension, breadth, and depth.

While his knowledge base was very deep, he never talked down to the person he addressed in his letters. To the contrary, he always minimized his stature in the correspondence. In this context my concern as translator was to carry the saint's seemingly fluid acquaintance with the writings of the Holy Fathers from the original nineteenth-century Russian into twenty-first century English while still conveying his often warm and humble tone of address.

The beauty of St Ignatius's written communication is what I would call his finely balanced verbal "aesthetics" for lack of more precise terms: his unique choice of imagery from nature, a gift for simile and metaphor, special tenderness of address that signals his love and affection for many who corresponded with him, an extensive knowledge of Holy Scriptures, his studied word order, and a gift for what he called "seeing souls."

Bishop Ignatius was often giving spiritual counsel in his letters. This was delivered with a voice of authority and at the same time, as a monastic and a man of deep Gospel faith, he couched his narrative in extremely humble terms. Each letter is a fine balance of all these elements and more.

I pray my efforts at translation are worthy of the original. If I missed the mark on occasion, I ask forgiveness. May the reader find here the spiritual consolation that was given me and my husband.

Elena Borowski

From My Hand and Heart: Selected Letters of St Ignatius (Brianchaninov)

∼ Trials ∼

You yourself know that no matter where one lives on the earth, trials must be endured. It often seems that we are tried by men, but without the permission of Providence, none of them could touch us. So while undergoing trials let us submit ourselves to the will of the Creator and consider ourselves deserving of our sorrows. If we do this we shall find rest.

Having passed through our trials does not mean that our external circumstances have changed, but rather that by submitting ourselves to the will of God and chiding ourselves, we gain patience. When we become very despondent and begin to complain about our trials, there is a danger of becoming an atheist, as one of our Holy Fathers said, and so becoming one with those who take arms against God's Providence. Forgive me Father! I speak to you, as I would to myself: since I often suffer from my own lusts and passions that draw me out and deceive me. Once deceived I give in to the resulting sin of grumbling, cowardice, and fury: I only achieve peace when I submit myself completely to the will of God. When I forget to glorify the Lord for all His good deeds and to give myself to His holy will and Providence, then a storm rises and the soul finds itself again in danger of drowning in the waves of cowardice and fear. If you struggle, then your way is not far from the road of God's righteous, who walk among many struggles. Having bloodied their feet they reach the Heavenly City of Jerusalem. There the sighs of suffering are not heard, but rather the constant joy of those who inherited the Heavenly Kingdom, having earned this with many sorrows.

Let us set aside, set aside, Father, our wish to find peace on this earth prematurely as it were, in order to receive it in time, that is, upon our death. Let us prepare the heart, with gratitude and praise, understanding that grief comes from the hand of God.[1]

◠ Remembrance of Death ◠

I do not abhor prisoners like yourself, as you write in your letter, knowing that I am in the chains of sin myself. And such an arrest, which is a sinful one, is the most tolerable, except a monastic needs to long for and hunger for such an arrest, because his disgrace and torments are eternal, except a sinful man will break out of these chains through repentance in good time.

The only thing left for you to do is to forsake all earthly concerns and prepare your soul for departure from its physical dwelling for life in heavenly realms. It is well known ahead of time that wherever we are found on this earth, whether on Valaam or in Optina, everywhere there are guests, everywhere wanderers, everywhere visitors, everywhere for a short while. Something else awaits us in eternity: there is always joy or always suffering.

The hour of death comes nigh! An impartial judgment awaits us, at which our deeds will be judged. The saints endlessly observe that their deeds are inadequate. As one of them said, they consider them-selves not fulfillers but ransackers of the commandments of the Lord; because of this when temptation comes, they rejoice, for through involuntary sorrow their deeds are augmented and their garments made white for their shame-free spiritual wedding at death's door. Enough, enough we have concerned ourselves with earthly things, with much time lost—and this day in the eleventh hour we will pre-pare for eternity. Our grumbling and worried voices we will change to words of gratitude and praise, for our Lord forges our salvation through unknown means and accomplishes it through small trials, not worthy of the name of sorrow. He humbles our blind will and by a single refraction of it through obedience He unites us to His all-wise Providence.[2]

∾ Good Deeds ∾

My travel exacerbated my illness, preventing me from doing what my heart felt was necessary.

I, as a sick man, should have as harbor for my hope not my works, not my merits, but the mercy and merits of the God-Man Jesus.

Jesus has prepared a hundredfold reward for good deeds and for those who do good the superfluous praise of men: and that is why we send a brief but sincere thank you for your love, kindness, and hos-pitality. In satisfying all the requirements of our heart, we leave aside compliments, those "garments" in which the false-hearted mostly dress, what might be called whore-flattery.[3]

∾ Struggles ∾

Anything done without a struggle becomes unreliable, and what you sow, and do not water with your tears, grows unpredictably. For-give me, Father, my idle chatter. I say this to you from the abundance of my heart and my involvement in these matters.[4]

◡ Sorrows ◡

Glory to God for all the sorrows which confront us! The person to whom sorrow is given is remembered by God in His Kingdom; the one who lives without sorrows is forgotten by God. By the multitude of sins that I fall into, Father, and by virtue of the many stupid things I do, there is no way I should judge the actions of my neighbor nor insist that anything be done this way or that.[5]

◡ Transience ◡

Our life is short. No matter what one acquires in this life, everything needs to be left behind upon our departure for eternity. One good thing which will leave with us is our love of the Lord and of our neighbor for God's sake. I pray to God that our love will last forever.

A certain Holy Father said that the sower sows in a row, but it is not known which grain will rise or which field will give the most bountiful harvest.

God is revealing to you the concept of monastic life that is Christian perfection. This is a gift from God; cultivate it. Using the natural goodness of your heart, together with the directness of your reason, acquire also the goodness of the Gospels and its way of thinking. May God, Who gave you excellent natural abilities, also give you Gospel-like love.

We live in deceptive times, no matter where we look, everywhere evil takes the lead, while well-meaning people live in oppression. The Saviour of the world commanded us to save our souls with patience. I rely on the will of God.

Prayer and the word of God—those are the only suitable studies for me. With the help of solitude these two directions, it seems from past efforts, will give me a chance to grow and prosper and that is how I hope to serve my neighbors.

Those who can speak the truth of Christ precisely, none can be found! The word of Christ is coming to pass: in the end days, will the Son of God find faith on earth?[6]

∿ Sorrows ∿

I congratulate you, my true friend, with the feast of this soul-saving monastery of ours. Our monastery has the blessed mercy of God upon it, because although there are not as many here as should be, there are people who have the intention of being pleasing to God. The Lord also sends temptations: he who belongs to God will be sent sorrows; the one for whom things go smoothly, like spreading butter, belongs to the devil. And when the Lord wishes to remove someone from the devil, he is charged with sorrows. Sorrows are Christ's chalice on the earth. Whoever is a partaker of this chalice on the earth will also partake of this chalice in Heaven. For us it is a source of endless delight. For fourteen years now we have been swimming together in the sea of life. There is no reckoning how these years passed by, nor will we see how the rest of our life will pass. If we examine this temporal life it only flatters—*blezir*,[7] as Russians say, and nothing more.[8]

∿ Formation ∿

Leave my arrival to the will of God; I have the following intention: I intend to leave this place, when I am assured that I have recovered and can embark upon travel safely, that when I reach you I will not just lie around but will be able to add to the common good. I admit lately it has weighed on my conscience, and I recognize the fact that I have not been engaged enough in instructing the brothers. I hope to resume this instruction as soon as the merciful Lord returns to me fresh strength. My eyes have improved so much that I am writing freely with the aid of light from a single candle. But I am still weak and am more likely lying down.

Your present position, even when accompanied by certain difficulties, forms your character. It strengthens you. I am very glad that God is so merciful that he has granted you a means to shape your life correctly on a straight and true path. Trouble comes when a person is formed along crooked paths: in a life whipped up through swindling.[9]

∼ Thorns ∼

My road, and those who want to accompany me, is strewn with thorns! By this path the Lord leads his chosen and His beloved. If a person is not led through the thorny path, their spiritual eyes will not open and they will not be able to see the blessings being given by Christ. Christ be with you. May He give strength both to you and to me.[10]

∼ Sorrows ∼

The merciful Lord, having chosen you for His own, allows different sorrows to come to you from both people and from physical illness. That is a blessed sign—receive it with a good-natured heart and with faith. When they shower you with insults and try to twist your words, remember that the same was done to Christ, and taste the cleansing chalice with a grateful heart.

God will allow you to taste the anguish that educates and makes you wise, in the very same way He did with me. Be generous in spirit: all temptations are only boogie men, lifeless marionettes, frightening only to those without faith, those who see only with their physical eyes. Be cautious, prudent before your mockers, imitate Christ's silence, and fear nothing. A hair from your head will not fall.[11, 12]

∼ Temptations ∼

Through the cleansing fire of sorrows and the purifying water of repentance it is appropriate for both soul and body to become refined like the silk of the spiderweb and to enter spiritual peace, the spiritual mind, and world of Christ, which is all one and the same.

Many of our good-hearted acquaintances, speaking kindly of us, have done us harm. We need to affectionately remind those who love us about this. However, when God is pleased to send us temptations, then they will come, issuing from sources we altogether thought impossible.

The Lord is unswervingly my Helper. A cunning politician thinks he is his own abettor. Similarly the Lord will not come to the aid of a person who relies on their own great intelligence. May the Lord enable me to see my own errors and do flee from them with repentance. Similarly, I do not wish to trouble myself about what someone may say: let them communicate what they wish. As for me, I urgently need to think about the life that is to come and my speedy departure there: such is promised to me by my premature aging and weakness, stemming from my long-term illnesses. I have no time to reach out and try to please people, those who consider only this present life on earth or who carry on as considering themselves eternal on this earth.

Congratulations on the Great Feast of the Annunciation. May the Mother of God receive us under Her roof! May she allow us to spend our earthly life in preparation for life eternal. The cup of sorrows discovers the potential treasures in each of us: David goes into the desert and Saul to the sorceress. God brought you to see by your own experience what kind of cup I drank in the Sergiev Hermitage during fourteen years. Stepping into the role of the Abbot of this monastery, I clearly saw, I would be grinding water, that my navigation will be along the abyss of intrigue: I was comforted by the thought that this was not by my choice. I gave myself to the will of God, to whom I still continue to give myself.[13]

⌒ Sorrows ⌒

I find myself unworthy of the confidence you have placed in me. When a person turns his gaze upon another during his struggles and extends his arms with trust asking for help he expects spiritual strength in return. I have no spiritual strength. I am bound by chains of passions, and am their slave, seeing only weakness in myself. But, having spent all my life in suffering, I consider it my duty to be compassionate to another who is suffering. I write you only from this motivation and only for this reason is my letter worthy of your attention. Accept this letter as a response of my soul, which participates in yours. In the solitude of sorrows even worthless participation is pleasant.

It is necessary for you to go by the narrow path of sorrows that the unfathomable ways of God have suddenly opened before you.

This circumstance is by no means unfamiliar to me. More than once I have seen the complete impoverishment of human assistance: not once was I betrayed by the ferocity of difficult conditions; not once was I under the power of my enemies. And do not think that my quandary lasted a short time. No! Years passed under these circumstances; physical health and strength dissipated, I weakened under the heavy burden of struggles, and the burden did not get lighter. Hardly did one sorrow pass than another appeared suddenly from a different quarter, and a new struggle settled heavily upon the soul, the soul already thin with the weight of a similar spiderweb, which preceded new trials.

Now I consider myself having lived half of the days of my life. I already see the opposite shore! My ever more intense weakness, the ever more frequent illnesses inform me of the closeness of my departure [to the next world]. I know not what storms still await me, but looking back, I sense in my heart an involuntary joy. Seeing many waves, through which my soul had to navigate, I am unexpectedly overjoyed. Heavy winds focused in on my soul; many unseen rocks awaited her, threatening her salvation, and still I survived. By human reckoning I should have died long ago. I am convinced that I was led by the strange and difficult paths of the inscrutable Providence of God; I am convinced that He stands watch over me as if holding my hand by His Almighty right hand. I submit myself to Him! May He lead me whither He wills; may He lead me, as He wishes, to a calm harbor, "where there is no sickness, nor sorrow, nor sighing."[14] I see many who are called happy and the price of their happiness is their lot to pay. Dead men lie in marble and wooden caskets with equal lack of feeling. Equally lacking in feeling they lie in magnificent monuments erected by vanity and ignorance of Christianity, as well as lacking in feeling for the humble wooden cross planted in faith and poverty. They are all victims of corruption.

The journey to the true knowledge of God will certainly require assistance from afflictions: we definitely need to mortify our heart to the world so that our heart can focus wholeheartedly on the search for God. When God chooses someone to become a vessel of spiritual gifts, for special close service to Himself, he will send him struggles (St Isaac the Syrian). Barely had God revealed Himself to Paul than He appointed for him a special destiny of suffering, "For I will show him how many things he must suffer for My name's sake" (Acts 9:16). People who cause grief and sorrowful circumstances are only instruments of the all-powerful right hand of God. All the hairs on your head are accounted for by God; not one of the mute birds fall without the will of his Creator; could any temptation come near you without His will? No! It came to you because it was allowed by God. The sleepless eye of Providence continually watches over you; His all-powerful right hand stands guard over you and directs your destiny. By permission or at His bidding, sorrows come to you as taskmasters over their victim. Your gold is cast into the furnace of temptations; it will emerge from the furnace cleaner and more valuable. People commit evil deeds out of blindness, but you commune with the Son of God on earth as well as in heaven. The Son of God tells His people: "You will indeed drink the cup that I drink" (Mark 10:39). Do not indulge in sorrow, cowardice, hopelessness! Say to your despondent thoughts—Most Honorable Father, to your heart pierced with sorrow—Tell your weary thoughts, "Shall I not drink the cup which My Father has given me?" (John 18:11) People who arbitrarily follow the promptings of the heart, who act willfully, still do not stop being instruments, blind instruments of Divine Providence, according to infinite and all-powerful Providence. Let us put people aside; surely they are outsiders! Having turned our gazes upon God, let us cast our rising and restless thoughts at His feet and say with awe and humility "Your will be done!" (Matt 6:10) And still that is not enough! Let us kiss the Cross, as a banner of Christ, which leads disciples of Christ to the Kingdom of Heaven. A thief was hung on the cross, as written in the Gospels, he was hung like a robber, but from the cross he was transported to heaven as a confessor. People pelted Stephen with stones, as a blasphemer, but by the judgment of God, Heaven parted for him as for a living temple of the Holy Spirit. St Tikhon of Voronezh, accused of having an irritable temper, was forced to leave his bishop's service and enter the walls of a silent monastery, whose stay there gave the appearance of being a place of exile for the holy shepherd, so he devoted himself to prayer and ascetic struggles. These holy monastic exercises earned him an incorruptible and abiding righteousness in Christ and glory from Him in Heaven and on earth. The fate of St Tikhon always amazed me; his example always shone as a consoling and guiding strength for my heart, when my heart was surrounded by gloom, accompanied by a gathering of clouds of sorrow. I am convinced that monastic exercises alone can console a man who finds himself in the jaws of temptation. I recommend to you the writings of St Mark the struggler, found in the first part of the *Philokalia*; they give spiritual comfort for one engaged in spiritual struggles; and for prayerful exercises, I recommend Hesychius, Filosofeya, and Feolipta, found in the second part of the same volume. Forgive me for allowing myself to advise you! Take it as a sign of my participation, as a sign of my sincerity, extracted from my soul with compassion for you. Otherwise I would not have entrusted you with secrets, which I conceal and which must be hidden in the depths of the soul, so that the priceless spiritual pearls not be stolen by those who love and value only their own morass. The unfolding in this letter of thoughts and ideas are concepts drawn from Holy Scriptures and compositions of the Holy Fathers, which nourished and sustained me. Without such powerful support, I could not have faced the afflictions sent to me by Divine Providence, which cut me off from love for the world and drew me to the love of God Himself. My sorrows with respect to my weakened health were not small and uncommon in our time. The fact that they could not break me right away only intensified and prolonged my suffering. Instead of breaking me in a few hours or days, the afflictions continued to work on me for many years. I see God's benevolence toward me in these sorrows; I profess a gift from above and thank God more for this blessing than for any visible earthly happiness which is imaginary. This imaginary happiness, no matter how low (for it is physical), might have been enviable if it were permanent and eternal. But it is unstable and momentary. And how tormented are people who are betrayed by it, who lose it, are spoiled by it. It will invariably be destroyed by relentless and inevitable death. There is nothing to compare with the devastation, when followers of earthly, imaginary love find themselves suddenly at the gates of eternity. St Isaac the Syrian said justly: "The World is a harlot: it attracts those who are predisposed to its beauty." He who gets caught in the love of the world cannot be freed from its clutches until he loses his life. The world strips man completely naked by drawing him from his home (i.e., his body) in the day of his death. Then the man learns that the world is a thief and a cheat.

Give me your hand: let us follow Christ, each carrying his own cross and through the cross each earns his own salvation.[15]

∽ The Cross ∽

Wherever I may be, whether in seclusion or in the society of people, light and consolation poured forth into my soul from the Cross of Christ.

Sin, taking possession of my whole being, does not cease to tell me "come down from the cross" (Matt 27:40, Mark 15:30).

Alas, I come down from the cross thinking I will find the truth away from it and fall into spiritual poverty: waves of embarrassment engulf me. I come down from the cross and then abide without Christ. How shall my spiritual poverty be corrected? I pray to Christ that He lift me back on the cross. While praying I attempt to crucify myself, as I have learned by previous experience that he who is not crucified is not of Christ. Faith lifts us upon the cross; corrupt reason takes us down through unbelief. As I conduct myself, so I advise my brothers also. What else can I add? "Blessed is the man who endures temptation" (Jas 1:12). "For in that He Himself has suffered, being tempted, He is able to aid those who are tempted" (Heb 2:18). I wish that these words from Holy Scripture come true for you as well. And you, take comfort! Do not be dismayed by the fact that you lost the battle: this adds to your spiritual skills or experience or humility. Peace be to you!

I must also say that the common way for ascetics is to heal one's infirmities through patient living among men, to behold God's Providence, and enter into inner prayer. Another person may take a different path, by special guidance from God, but most of us must take the common path. Read about this in the fifty-fifth word of St Isaac to St Simeon the Wonderworker. Some say that solitude is the quickest means to spiritual success; and others still say that what brings ascetic gains is love of one's neighbor. My heart is more inclined toward the latter, because love of one's neighbor is the indispensable duty of each of us; and very few are capable of silence.[16]

∼ Remembrance of Death ∼

Blessed be the Lord, who facilitated your transition from a self-willed lifestyle to another, closer to the tradition of the Holy Fathers. One who practices silence is somehow not accustomed to verbosity even in the most prayerful rule. Although all men are created in the image of God, in this case the practitioner of silence is a most special, most true image of God. Look at what John the Evangelist says about God: from all eternity He contented himself with a Single Word! The consolation that I hope for in the mercy of God will emerge from your present ascetic efforts will confirm this truth in you. In time, truth will demand that you shed even more leaves to reveal the fruit of your labors.

It is useful to compel oneself to remembrance of death, even if the heart turns from thoughts of this. Our remembrance of death is a gift of God and compelling ourselves to her is just a witness to the sincerity of our wish to have this. As we compel ourselves we need to pray: "Lord, give me remembrance of death."

Such is the teaching on the subject by Macarius the Great, Isaac the Syrian, and similar great Fathers. You will find this topic in the priceless book of Nil Sorsky. About the love of our neighbor we know from the teachings of the Fathers that it is of two kinds: natural love and Gospel love, or the love of Christ. The natural kind of love is implanted in us from our creation and that is why it most certainly exists in each of us. Our natural love is damaged together with other good qualities by the fall of Adam and Eve or our ancestral sin; and that is why each person is subject to more or less short or long-term changes. Christ who heals all ailments in marvelous ways also heals our damaged love; He commands that we love Him, the Lord Himself in other people. Thus He raises love to the highest degree of fervor, gives her purity, spirituality, and sanctity. With the flame of love of Christ He extinguishes the discordant, smoky flame of carnal love that contains admixtures of dreaminess, nonexistent delights, and cruel murderous suffering. The sensation of spiritual love led the pen of St John of the Ladder, when he said: "Love of God extinguishes the flame of love for parents and others close by birth; he who says he has one and the other kind of love deceives himself." John of the Ladder also said in the fifteenth step: "Fire quenches fire, that is love of God extinguishes carnal love." When we see ourselves attentively, we shall see with God's help (such eyesight needs God's help! Such vision is a gift of God!) The more we have natural love, the greater is our need to acquire Gospel love. I understood this myself, when I wrote you that the Gospel of Matthew precedes the Gospel of John; the Gospel of John speaks more about the love of God, about seeing God, which is clear only for those who have been cleansed. When a man becomes purified, he enters into seeing God and love for Him through the love of one's neighbor through Christ or the love of Christ in each neighbor. But those who are estranged from Christianity and Christ we should love for the image of God in them. And he who is deprived of the glory of Christianity is not deprived of the glory of mankind, being made in the image of God!

You appealed to me in the name of God for the good of your soul; I also in the name of God am inclined to speak to you about that which I consider true and good for your soul. I journey toward the Lord by way of the mind and heart, wishing to stand before His majestic unapproachable glory face to face. Do not be coldly rational and multisyllabic. He is more pleased with the babble of a young soul, humbling itself, so to speak, by seeing multitudes of its infirmities, rather than eloquent preenings of the soul, puffed up by self-conceit. The Apostle Paul said about himself: "For I determined not to know anything among you except Jesus Christ and Him crucified" (1 Cor 2:2).

And for me it is sufficient to see that I am a sinner. This knowledge will be enough for me! It pierces my hard heart like Moses's staff in the stone and draws from me living stream of tears. My cry before the Lord I prefer to all earthly wisdom "and my sin is ever before me" (Ps 50:3). My sin is the preeminent object of my spiritual contemplation![17]

⌇ Remembrance of Death ⌇

What can be more difficult than the condition of the soul tormented by temptations? This is like being in hell, under eternal torment. The remembrance of these lightens our current temptations. It says in the Ladder[18] that the remembrance of death is the enemy of despondency. Think what the company of demons in hell will be like and people will appear kind to you by comparison; remember the torments in hell and temptations will appear light to you.

If your thoughts stray from the example given to us by the recluse with humility, then listen to the advice of holy John of the Ladder, speaking in the fourth stage of his Ladder, like this: "Those who make easy decisions to move from place to place are not very clever: because nothing makes the soul so non-productive as lack of patience . . . By moving, you could lose that redemption, which Christ prepared for you." St Gregory of Sinai likens those who move from place to place to transplanted trees: with each transplanting they are in danger of perishing and most certainly they lose a significant measure of their strength.

Regarding the prayer rule know that it is for you (not you for it) and for the Lord. That is why you have freedom to reason about it. When you are weak, shorten it; when you feel stronger, add to it— the one and the other with moderation and caution because we are extremely infirm and surrounded by snares and killers of the spirit. When you are not in church, then read the prayer rule, written out by you: I approve it, at least for now, until my wretched heart receives a message from you to change it.

It is forbidden to pray for heretics, as though they were members of the Church, nor to take a portion of the holy bread prosphoron the image of participation in the Church, but pray for their conversion; that is allowed. He who has an image of his own corpse cries over him, prays for him. Prisoners behind bars cannot take upon themselves efforts to save other prisoners. The Lord is Love, and He has a powerful wish to save everyone, something we cannot even grasp. Let us offer that Love for our own salvation and for others. And on our part let us try (and that depends on us) to purify ourselves. We will achieve this when we mortify ourselves to the world. Glory to God![19]

∼ Struggles ∼

If you ascribe only joy to my sinful heart when I hear that my spiritual children walk in truth, then why should I ascribe sorrow for your silence, for not receiving thankful words from you, which belong to God alone. To Him alone prayers are raised on wings, on the wings of sighs from the heart. The Truth is our Lord Jesus Christ. Standing humbly before Pilate who questions Him about Truth, looking at It, and not recognizing It. In the same manner today the servants of this world look upon Truth, and see It not; listen to It, and hear It not. This is Divine Truth, who came down on earth to fallen and infirm men, men of whom it is said "their heart is joined to evil from their youth."[20]

As long as man is damaged, he is subject to inevitable change-ability, a result of our ancestors' fall, up to his last breath on earth. Thus it is no wonder you see in yourself ceaseless changeability: do not expect to be rid of it before dying; better not deceive yourself with this hope. If you do troubles will always find you in disarray, acting upon you with even more powerful force, even subverting you. Marvel and bow before Truth, which ceaselessly heals human changeability with the commandment of constant repentance. Lying down on your bed, repent, and upon rising repent; as one link in a chain holds another, so in your life one sigh follows another. Thus you spend days, months, and years. The subject of your reflections should be your infirmities. Sensations of your heart will be like one plunged into a dungeon, similar to a leper, exiled outside his camp. Your suffering will cease when your life ceases; your last moan will be emitted with your last gasp. For a monk consolation on this earth comes with tears and tender emotion. What tears? That is the action of grace, given you during baptism; this is the movement of the Holy Spirit planted in you, a sinner, during holy baptism; that is why holy tears are not present in those who know not Christ, neither in here-tics. Do you wish to feel relief from passions that struggle within you? As you live in your cell, do you wish to find tender emotion, with-out which one is a boat without an anchor, sent rushing through the waves of dreams and crashes in the depths of despondency? Do you wish to see light from the Light? Do you wish to taste love coming from Love and leading to Love? Take your thoughts and cast them at the feet of your brothers and sisters, without distinguishing the bad from the good; speak your thoughts as often as possible, so that these would give birth to the feeling: "these are Divine Angels, and I alone in my darkness and sin am like the devil." ... You are destined to find relief for your soul at the feet of your brothers; the prayer of the publican[21] is chosen for you, and not the Jesus Prayer. The Kingdom of Heaven is cast open for you by the confession of the robber, not by the relics of John. Well up from the heart and say: "Hearken, O daughter, and see, incline thine ear" (Ps 44:11). Likewise when you adorn yourself with repentance, then "the King shall greatly desire thy beauty" (Ps 44:12), which issues from your repentance.

You write about your stream of thoughts and wish to understand them and find out what the apostle means by the words "to carry our struggle" and so forth. This is not profitable for you and not needed. It is sufficient for you to know that any minute you can be accosted by your own passions and unclean spirits wishing your downfall. As one who is infirm, you must constantly cry to our Lord: "Have mercy upon me, for I am weak!" (Ps 6:2) The Lord will be your salvation when your devotion makes Him your fortress and your ascetic exercises make Him your song. "The Lord is my strength, and my song, and is become my salvation" (Ps 117:14). Then you will not die but will live through repentance and lead the work of the Lord as He extracts sinners from hell and leads them to Paradise. Oh, when will the Lord grant this! Be prepared for struggles and they will become light; refuse to be comforted and rest will come to the one who considers himself unworthy of it.[22]

∽ Tears ∽

God grants me the task of messenger to you about the death of your brother, which happened the day after Theophany. He made his confession while still fully conscious and partook of the mystery of Holy Communion. Two hours later he lost the power of speech. That is all that your heart needs to know.

May streams of tears pour comfort for those who remain and those who are departed. May your prayers shine in the drops of tears, like the drops of rain form multicolored rainbows. This is an image or more correctly a symbol of peace between God and mankind. May your prayer likewise be of many colors: confession, contrition of the heart, repentance, tenderness, and joy. A rainbow is a joyful arc. May your prayer be like this arc. One end of the rainbow touches your heart and the other end the sky. May the light of hope and expectations shine in your soul, light from the Light—of Christ, Who washed our sins and redeemed us from the darkness of sin. We entrust ourselves and each other to Him, just as His mercy rests upon you. Amen.[23]

∽ Harvest ∽

I see a spiritual harvest in you, which consists in the knowledge of your own weaknesses. St Paul the apostle spoke about infirmities: "Therefore most gladly I will rather boast in my infirmities, that the power of Christ may rest upon me" (2 Cor 12: 9).

Be guided by your conscience. After reading this letter, take notice what feelings are there in your soul? If you detect peace and calm spreading there, then know that what was told you was also told to the Lord; your conscience will be a witness to you that what was said to Christ must come to pass, even if it is interwoven with sorrow. The Holy Fathers said that virtues are nothing without struggles. The Lord speaks in the Gospels (Luke 8:5–15) explaining the parable about the seeds that fell on different soils: "But the ones *that* fell on the good ground are those who, having heard the word with a noble and good heart, keep *it* and bear fruit with patience." Having said this the Lord added these terrible words: "He who has ears to hear, let him hear!" (Luke 8:8). I also ask—look into your heart—and you will find that you had a sacred desire, according to your strength, to bring spiritual benefit to any sister. Through God's foreknowledge this has all been settled, though not the way our imagination designed it, but in His. What we imagined to be beneficial turned out to be fruitless and that which we imagined to be harmful and weak produced the most fruitful harvest. The glory for the harvest belongs to the One God, and we find ourselves only with our weaknesses, in a debt that cannot be paid back to God! I invite you: with our reasoning and heartfelt feelings, let us descend into nothingness. May Christ be exalted in us and let us mortify what is of the flesh and this world in us. A dead person is devoid of life and without action. Let us mortify ourselves, so Christ can live and act through us. Be merciful to your soul in Her infirmities; excessive strictness distracts from repentance and leads to depression and despair. Remain at peace with your circumstances, attending to the end of your management of your estate: Christ's commandment requires this of you, assuring you that "you cannot serve God and mammon" (Matt 6:24). May peace be with you. Amen.[24]

～ Self-Reproach ～

May the Lord comfort your grieving heart! While we are on our journey and before we enter the harbor of changeless eternity, we should expect for ourselves and in our circumstances change, ordinary and unexpected upheavals and sorrows. A certain venerable Father said: "Glory to God for all things, even our very infirmities! For it is preferable to be a sinner and recognize this, than it is to be superficially righteous and consider oneself as such." These words are extremely comforting to those of us who are weak and sinful. They do not provide occasion to sin freely but console those who take heed of themselves and sense that their soul is an involuntary captive of sin. Reflecting upon this and seeing the absence of truth in the affairs of our life, we need to acquire the repentance of the publican: a contrite and humble heart that the Lord does not despise.[25] Do not blame anyone for your infirmities or even the circumstances and diversions you find yourself in. Blame yourself exclusively. King David, the holy prophet, the God-seer Moses and the saint and prophet Daniel pleased God amidst a multitude of activities and a diversity of entertainments. St John of the Ladder describes venerable saints living in the monastic communities of Egypt who told him "acquire stillness of mind among the noise of human chatter and that is glorious." Reproach yourself, specifically your feeble will, because the power of volition in those who are weak produces great things! You will discover comfort in reproaching yourself. Reproach and judge yourself and God will justify and have mercy upon you. When Patriarch Theophilus of Alexandria arrived at a monastery in the Nitreian mountains, he asked the abbot, under whose supervision up to 10,000 monks were being saved: "What, Father, did you find to be especially important in monastic life? 'Reproach and judge yourself ceaselessly', responded the holy abbot. 'Yes' agreed the patriarch, as there is no other means for salvation." And you also need to acquire this easy labor, capable of bringing humility into your soul. From such self-reproach will follow consolation and peace from the Lord, and rest in Him after the labors of a burdened heart. I wish you peace, spiritual consolation, and your salvation.[26]

～ The Cross ～

Your way of your life lies along narrow paths and sorrows, as it is promised to all who follow Christ. Those who follow Him like the matchless Peter and the first-called Andrew are destined for the cross. The cross is also the destiny of the one who addresses Christ like the thief. In the first case the cross is the result of a crown, in the second case a ladder. No matter what the circumstance, to which model applies to us, you cannot belong to Christ without the cross, "And so I am ready always to take upon myself any sorrow which Providence sends my way."[27] May the Lord strengthen you.[28]

～ Trials ～

You are entering the sea of monasticism on the vessel of faith. With this faith you are transported over the waves of the monastic sea; these comprise a variety of trials, allowed by God's Providence for our salvation, brought about both by our own shortcomings and by our enemy the devil. I am comforted by the thought that you are being tonsured. May the Lord bless and strengthen you![29]

∼ Self-Reproach ∼

It is a blessing to be a monk or nun, who has lived for a long time in a monastery and reached old age. Such a person can spend the rest of their days taking heed of themselves, in silence, in preparation for the transition into eternity. Those who wish to piously and successfully practice silence must lay a foundation of constant self-reproach in their life, as was said by the great elder of the Nitreian mountain, Theophilus, Patriarch of Alexandria. I ask your holy prayers for me to the Lord that He may grant me that labor, which I indicated to you, without which it is impossible for the soul to calm down and escape from the state of confusion and distraction.[30]

∼ Service ∼

Labor with patient consistency in the manner of the blessed Martha, who was chosen to prepare and deliver food for the Saviour. Await faithfully your rewards from the Lord. He will say to those who served their brothers at His last judgment: "Assuredly, I say to you, inasmuch as you did *it* to one of the least of these My brethren, you did *it* to Me" (Matt 25:40).

And the Lord will lead him who served his brothers assiduously into eternal peace and the joy of heaven. Remember that the cup of cold water does not lose its recompense in Heaven: do not miss opportunities for increasing your rewards. Keep in mind that you are not serving people but Angels, and so your service will become sweet. Give your love and service to your neighbor for God's sake and not for your heart, impulsively or by choice. Avoid especially any bias and you will be purified for your service: it will be a sacrifice acceptable to God.

Take care not to hurt your neighbor. St Anthony the Great said: "From our neighbor comes our life or death: If we please our brother, God will be pleased. Conversely if we offend our brother we sin against Christ Himself." So guard against offending your brothers! Any service or offense made toward one's neighbor is received by Christ as if it were done to Him, the Lord. If you have to refuse your brother in something do so softly but with firmness, explaining why you cannot fulfill his wish. If you should become involved and sin in something by virtue of your human infirmity do not fall into despair. To the contrary, run to the Lord with your repentance and you shall be forgiven. Christ is with you. Pray for me, who loves you much in the Lord.[31]

∼ Storms ∼

The journey of life is likened to swimming a vast sea. This sea is sometimes quiet and sometimes has a tailwind blowing, but most often it is tempestuous. Seeing the oncoming storm, the tempest itself, we must not fall into despondency and despair. We must stand up to the waves, resist the contrary wind. Otherwise the ship of our soul may become devastated, even submerged. If during a storm something should break or become damaged in our ship of the soul, we must not despair or be embarrassed. One needs to look out for a trustworthy harbor, enter it, make repairs of what was damaged, then continue on our journey hoping in the Almighty God. The Almighty God will not abandon the person who places his hopes in Him! Storms themselves will serve as a benefit to the faithful servant of Christ: they will make him a more skillful swimmer. The harbors where the ship of our soul is repaired are prayer in a humble spirit, reading the Holy Scriptures and books of our Holy Fathers, and seeking counsel from our neighbor (if the neighbor is capable of giving advice in the Lord). Calm down: "Blessed is the man," the Scripture tells us, "who endures temptation" (Jas 1:12). On the contrary, those who have not been tempted are not skillful. May the past storm serve to prepare and aid you in enduring future tempests. Consider in advance what should be your conduct in future storms, study and prepare well in advance. Because storms will certainly follow. Our Wise Lord has preordained that we should experience tribulations before we enter the Kingdom of Heaven, which we lost and continue to lose through our timeless and impermissible pursuit of pleasure. We are all like our forefather, inclined to extend our bold hand toward the forbidden fruit of the knowledge of good and evil. We are prone to receive comfort from the physical world, easily charmed by the deceitful specter of spiritual discussions and virtue, under whose mask hides deadly evil which kills us. Grief has an opposite effect to pleasure; that is why it counteracts our fallen state and promotes our restoration. Because of these properties, sorrow is necessary for our salvation. For reasons of necessity, our Saviour led His holy flock through a path of trials in order to reach blessed eternity. To anyone who refuses His trials, he declares emphatically: "And he who does not take his cross and follow after Me is not worthy of Me" (Matt 10:38).[32]

∼ Repentance ∼

You are traveling to Jerusalem, to those places that were the earthly habitation of Christ the Saviour. He said of these to the Samaritan woman: "Woman, believe Me, the hour is coming when you will neither on this mountain, nor in Jerusalem, worship the Father[. . . .]But the hour is coming and now is, when the true worshipers will worship the Father in spirit and truth; for the Father is seeking such to worship Him" (John 4:21). Another thought comes to mind about circumstances in Jerusalem, of which the paralytic complained to the Lord: "Sir, I have no man to put me into the pool when the water is stirred up" (John 5:7). I also would like to be in Jerusalem! I see Him in the Gospels. Even now Christ lives there, having said to His followers: "And lo, I am with you always, even to the end of the age" (Matt 28:20). Into that Jerusalem there is but one gate: repentance! I want to go through that gate! I would not wish to stay outside. I would not want to be caught on the way as night fell! During the night outside the city, beasts of prey wander about! The tardy traveler conveniently becomes a victim . . . There a parable was told of the foolish virgins who arrived late at the gate. They were left outside the gate hearing only a voice from inside: "I never knew you; depart from Me you who practice lawlessness!" (Matt 7:23).

Here are the thoughts that came to me involuntarily at the news of your journey to Jerusalem. This news saddened me. St John of the Ladder said about our monastic road: "Woe unto him who is alone . . . for where two or three are gathered in My name, there am I in the midst of them" (Step 26). What a pity that the good companion leaves for a distant land! His good word and good deeds will be hidden from us by great distance and will no longer benefit us! I am comforted by the fact that we are all at the mercy of God, that God's Providence protects us, invisibly holds His sincere servants by the hand on the way to His holy desires. What can I tell you for the road? The same thought I repeat constantly: let us immerse ourselves in repentance, let us remain there, let us clean our garments with it. God will certainly do His part as those who have been cleansed with repentance He enlightens with the grace of the Holy Spirit.

I wish you prosperous travel. Please do not cease your love for me a sinner! I ask your holy prayers for me a sinner![33]

∽ Sorrows ∽

Having bowed before the wing of thoughts and feelings, I stand reverently before you. I was taught to stand so reverently by angels, who gaze in awe, according to the Scriptures, on the suffering of Christ's servants. Indeed it is a wonderful sight obliging us to stand in reverence: how flesh and blood are trampled by flesh and blood. I ask for your holy prayers because "the eyes of the Lord are over the righteous, And His ears are open unto their prayers" (Ps 33:16).

The reverend Moses of Scetis once saw how the Holy Spirit came down upon the young monk Zachariah. He realized that Zachariah's tongue became the pen of the fast-writing Spirit and asked, "tell me, how should I conduct myself?" Zachariah took off the *kamilavka*[34] from his head, put it under his feet, stepped on it and said: "If the man in you does not get crushed you cannot become a monk." Whoever keeps death (the inevitable destiny of each person) and eternity before his eyes will laugh at both the sorrows and sweetness of this world. He whose memory of death and eternity is stolen by the enemy will have his temporal life grow into eternal life and his sorrows multiply into countless, irresistible giants. Once the monk remembers death, these giants crumple into dust; the curtain that hid eternity from him is turned aside and before him events of this world appear like the amusements and punishment of children!

Into eternity! Into eternity we fly through life! Everything sweet and bitter remains behind us. The past seems to never have happened. Only eternity is not subject to time nor change. It should be recognized as substantial, worthy of all our attention, worthy of all our care, because it remains forever. The devil tries to divert our vision, so we might lose track of eternity. When eternity has slipped away from our vision man fights and struggles in the net of the catcher. Spiritual intelligence, that is humility, cuts through this net. "Remember the time you will die, and you will never sin" (Sir 7: 36). Neither shall you murmur against the blessed yoke of Christ, nor against exhaustion in the coveted and glorious struggle of a monastic. "But he who endures to the end will be saved" (Matt 10:22). "But if anyone draws back," announces God, "My soul has no pleasure in him" (Heb 10:38).[35]

⟑ Sorrows ⟑

May the Lord bless your intentions and say "thou knewest my paths"(Ps 141:4). Having torn apart your heart with sorrows and crushed and shattered it with temptations from men, the Lord will sow it with seeds of His Truth and comfort you with spiritual fruits.[36]

⸺ Struggles ⸺

I see the wonderful hand of God upon you! You are under the affliction of the cross and your children, the fruit of your womb, also bring their shoulders to the cross of Christ, having rejected the yoke of the world as useless! My mother was much upset at my entry into the monastery, but on her death bed, several minutes before her end, she said, "Now at this time, I have one consolation: my oldest son—is in the monastery." I often think what inexplicable grief will grip some parents at the last judgment of Christ: those parents whom Christ the impartial judge will reprove and condemn for sacrificing their children to the world and the master of the world! What incomparable joy will embrace those parents whom this Judge will bless and praise for bringing their offspring as a sacrifice to God, for preparing them to live in illuminated paradise.

That kind of joy awaits you! Two wreaths await you: one for your personal struggles and another for your children. Wonderful are these wreaths of joy! Would you not wish to try them on! They are given to you in the next life but you can try them here if you want to. Would you like this? By the grace of God I will teach you how to catch them. They are refined, spiritual: not everyone knows how they are caught and how to try them out. Set yourself a goal to thank the Lord daily for your cup, that is for your infirmities, for all your struggles, for the lot of your daughters; your sorrowful thoughts are especially dissipated by thanking God; when such thoughts come to you, "thanksgiving" is voiced in plain words, with attention and often, until your heart feels relief. Sorrowful thoughts bring no benefit: sorrows are not diminished, they bring no help but just upset your body and soul. This means they are from demons and need to be chased away. Sorrowful thoughts are chased away by thanksgiving to God.

Giving thanks calms the heart, bringing consolation and finally heavenly joy. Such is a pledge and foretaste of joy eternal. If you will give thanks your reward will be suited to you. I would like to see your soul, wearing a Heavenly wreath, a wreath of blessed joy of the soul! Thanksgiving is among the few simple words, but it bears more fruit than thousands of the wisest books. Giving thanks is a weapon, bequeathed to Christians by the Holy Spirit through the Apostles. Giving thanks is apostolic, God's gift and inheritance. Giving thanks to God performs miracles and wonders! These wonders are not seen by physical eyes but by the incomparably excellent inner eyes of the soul that are part of our spiritual framework: there thanks to the Divine touch the painful fire leaves Peter's mother-in-law.[37] Peter is the image of faith, his mother-in-law of the soul, the nearest relative to Peter.

Thanksgiving is all-powerful for God Almighty to whom it is offered! Thanksgiving is powerful through faith, which alone, decidedly alone, is capable of receiving and embracing the infinite power of God; faith has no boundaries, just as there are no limitations to God and all that is related to God. Reason, no matter how reasonable, is useless for the works of God.[38]

∼ Sufferings ∼

Today Christians suffer not from shackles and swords; let us endure the torture of illnesses and other afflictions. Each historic period has its own kind of suffering; in our time we are given to suffer trifles. Let us tolerate them. The scales of justice and revenge are with God.

Why should you have bitterness? "Mercy and truth are met together, justice and peace have kissed each other" (Ps 84:11), the Scriptures say: Where there is no "mercy," there is "bitterness." When there is no "Truth" there is no "peace," there is no "justice." And the state of the soul, which lacks Divine Truth and Justice, cannot be called "a condition from God." One must rid the soul of this status and bring to the soul a condition that gives us Divine Truth and Justice: a condition of "Peace and Mercy." You will succeed in this if you say to yourself: "Whatever happens to me is not without Divine Providence. Blessed be the name of God from now and forever." Do not peer into life's

circumstances too much: they are not worth it. They rush by, changing one after another.[. . .] And we also are hastening to the edge
of eternity! Those who stare at these circumstances and consider
them unmoving may easily fall into despondency. Whoever sees that
everything is hurtling through time, and that he himself is flying, will
find things easier to bear and discover joy in his heart.[39]

~ Sorrows ~

When over the gloomy and deep abyss of grief, sorrows suddenly
open before us, carry on up on the wings of faith! Do not be moved by
disbelieving waves of human thoughts. Walk boldly over them with the
courageous steps of your faith and under your feet they will turn from
soft, moist waves into solid marble or granite plates. Furthermore,
timidity and doubt do not suit you. As you look upon the powerful
winds there is one who calls upon you to walk among the sorrowful
seas that separate you from your brethren: It is the Lord Himself. This
calling is also a blessed election! Christ marks "His own" with the seal
of suffering. He found your soul useful for Himself and that is why He
marks it with his seal! And the small flock stands out, as part of Christ,
from among other people; Christ's flock holds in its hands the sign of
being chosen by Christ, the cup of Christ. On their shoulders there is a
banner: the Cross of Christ. Far, far were they flung from the children
of the world!

The measureless crowd, with noise and in strange rapture, chase
after temporary comforts and pleasures. Time, in their sight, has been
transformed into eternity! They spend their careless lives, succeeding
only at things that decay. Forgotten by God they do not attract the
antagonism of the devil, because they are pleasing the devil and are
a part of him. Christ's chalice opens the way for the spiritual mind
that is the spiritual state. Those who enter and take the Communion
meal of comfort become dead to the world, senseless to temporary
tribulations and deprivations. They begin their earthly pilgrimage, so
to speak, carried in the air above everything on the wings of faith. The

fetters of the mind pull us toward the earth, the country of torment; being on the earth we cannot help but be exposed to torments. As is written in the Scripture, "For in the abundance of wisdom there is abundance of knowledge. And he who increaseth knowledge will increase suffering" (Eccl 1:18). Faith lifts us from the earth, frees us of the shackles of sorrows, raises us up to Heaven, and leads us to spiritual comfort. Those who enter this peace rest in cool comfort, taking delight on luxuriously covers, precious resting places within visions of God.

Here is an irreconcilable war, there is an endless battle, a bloody struggle between the Israelites and foreign nations. Among the foreigners who stand against Israel are the giants, the sons of Anak, sorrows that bring us fear, paralysis, and despair. The spy of Israel that is intelligence proclaims to her soul and forces: "The land through which we went as spies is a land that devours its inhabitants, and all the people we saw in it are of great stature" (Num 13:32). Exactly! Reasoning, based on a common course of things, thoughts substantially and only human in origin brings "And there we saw the giants; and we seemed like grasshoppers to them, but so we actually were" (Num 13:33). But the true Israelite is faithful to God, is guided by faith in God; he is equipped with complete armor.

"I will pursue mine enemies, and overtake them, neither will I turn back, until they are dead. I will smite them, and they shall not be able to stand; they shall fall under my feet. For Thou hast girded me with strength unto the battle; Thou hast crushed under me them that rose up against me. Thou hast made mine enemies also to turn their backs upon me, and thou hast utterly destroyed them that hated me. They cried, but there was none to save them; even unto the Lord, and He did not hear them. I will grind them down as the dust before the face of the wind; I will trample them as mud in the streets" (Ps 17:38–43). Not endorsed in this war are the many and subtle reflections, which the mind tries to force, enamored of itself, on its own powers, relying on the quantity and reach of its own knowledge, resisting the crowds of pressing strangers that are foreign thoughts. "The children of Ephraim, being armed and carrying bows" announces the Prophet–"turned back in the day of battle" (Ps 77:9). Human reason cannot resist the thick legions of foreign thoughts! They will mislead, producing resentment and confusion in the mind!—Then victory is on their side!

For certain success in the invisible battle with the lords of the air, with evil spirits and dark forces one needs armor, given to us by faith and by the power of Christ. "Because the foolishness of God is wiser than men, and the weakness of God is stronger than men" (1 Cor 1:25). The reasonings and teachings of faith are strange and terrifying to the earthly mind; but no sooner shall man see in his own experience, glimpse with his own inner sensations, the power of faith, then he will instantly and happily submit to its lead. He will be as one who has received a priceless mentor and turns away with contempt from the human wisdom that has been rejected by God.

Here are the weapons that the words of Christ's teaching give to the servant of Christ for battle with the sons of Anak[40]: the battle against dark thoughts and feelings of sadness that confront the soul in images of fearsome giants ready to wipe out and swallow it:

First, "Glory to God for everything."
Second, "Lord! I surrender to Thy Holy Will! May your Holy Will be done."
Third, "Lord! Thank You for everything, that You were pleased to send me."
Fourth, "According to my deeds I will accept all; remember me, Lord, in Your Kingdom."

These brief words, borrowed, as you see, from the Scriptures, were used by holy monks with excellent success against foreign thoughts of despondency. The Fathers never reasoned with the dark thoughts that appeared to them; no, no sooner did the foreign strange thought appear than they grabbed their wonderful weapon and shoved it in the face, right in the jaw of the stranger! That is why they were so strong, trampled all their enemies, became warriors of faith, and by means of faith became instruments of grace and accomplished super-natural feats.

At the appearance of depressing thoughts or longings in your heart, immediately grasp your weapon, and from the bottom of your heart, speak one of the above phrases; enunciate it quietly, without haste, without heat, with complete attention, loud enough for your hearing alone. Speak this phrase until the foreign thought disappears completely and your heart senses the arrival of the Divine Grace to assist you. This Grace arrives in your soul as a sweet, comforting peace, the peace of the Lord, and for no other reason whatsoever. In time the strange thoughts will again approach you, but grab your armor once more, as the ingenious leader, Caesar, told his troops, aim directly for the face of the enemy: no other part of the body is so damaging as a strike in the face. Do not wonder at the strangeness or apparent uselessness of the weapon of David[41]! Use it in your own battle and you will see the sign! These weapons, the mace and the stone, will win more battles than all the collected, deep-thinking judgments and rare theories of theologians or of any wordsmiths, whether German, Spanish, English, or American! Using these weapons in your work will gradually transform you from the path of reason to the path of faith, and this will lead you into the immense and marvelous country of the spirit. There one is served manna as the hidden meal; to this land Christ admits only the victorious. You are brought into this unseen warfare in order to become a victor, and in this state you inherit spiritual treasure. All this Christ gives you, having loved you, clearly counting you among "his own."

Gazing from the very shore of this dark, deep sea of sorrows, upon the distance, the azure of the sea merges with the azure of the heavens. Looking at this dark, boundless expanse that frightens faith, I listen to the angry murmur of the waves, to their monotonous and unfeeling splashing, but do not indulge in melancholy or permit this sad sea of thoughts in my soul. There is more peril here! It is easier to drown here in this interior sea than in the exterior sea of sorrows.

You are on the seashore of sorrows in order to swim to the opposite shore of joys: the other shore is there, even though it is invisible to the eyes of human reason. That shore is an inner heaven, replete with spiritual delights. Those who reach this forget, in their ecstasy of pleasure, all the grief endured by them in the sea. Step fearlessly into the light ferry of faith and be carried as by wings over the wet hillocks! Faster than you imagine, you shall be carried over the sea, transported into paradise. But between spiritual paradise and earthly carnal and ordinary life, where most people reside, there lies the vast sea that is the cross and the crucifixion. There is no other way to heaven! Whomever God wants to elevate into heaven, that person first begins his path to heaven through the cross. "The sign of God's election, wrote one ascetic Father, is when endless sorrows encompass a man." Let us endure the sorrows that mortify our life on earth, in order to become worthy of receiving the living God, with the help of the real, fully perceptible aid of the Spirit. Let us endure the decay of this world in order to acquire the Spirit! Surrender to God completely! Cast yourself into the saving abyss of faith, as if into a sea from a high rock!

Leave people behind as instruments of Providence! They are blind instruments themselves who have no power, no movement! "You could have no power at all against Me," said the Lord to Pilate, "unless it had been given you from above" (John 19:11). While Pilate, led by the judgment of men, admitted and argued (and with this, without any doubt each person agreed with him in his judgment) that he has power to crucify the Prisoner standing before him, as well as the power to release Him. Do not be concerned about any contacts with people, nor trouble yourself with explanations before them! Such interactions and explanations only disrupt the peace in your heart and will not bring any benefit. Frail people are like flowers that appear for a short time on the surface of the earth! You dream a lot about yourself, you ascribe a lot to yourself, but you are all frail people! You honor yourself with self-rule, and nonetheless you do not cease to be instruments, blind instruments, tools of others! And you cannot see and thus do not know that you are instruments! You are autocratic, that is so! "You cannot but take bribes for your own deeds." But by virtue of the infinite wisdom of God these independent ones are actors without the least bit of power, without any autonomy. "Jesus of Nazareth," said the Apostle Peter to the Jews, "Him, being delivered by the determined purpose and foreknowledge of God, you have taken by lawless hands, have crucified, and put to death" (Acts 2:23). "I know that you did it in ignorance, as did also your rulers. But those things which God foretold by the mouth of all His prophets, that the Christ would suffer, He has thus fulfilled" (Acts 3:17–18). In matters concerning God's Providence, people are blind. That is why the Lord did not count people worthy, apparently bereft of all power, to have any answers! That is why He called up the chalice, prepared by evil-wishers, demons, and bodiless spirits, as the cup given by God himself.

Please accept these lines as an echo of the soul, which participates with you and has sincere compassion in your sorrows and earnestly wishes you receive consolation from our Lord.[42]

∾ Prayer ∾

You write that "you do not always practice your cell rule either through weakness, or because you are distracted by visitors, and then you feel sorrow." In reply to that I repeat, that the person is not for the rule, but the rule is for the person. That is why, when you have sinned by reason of weakness of the flesh, or of the soul, or by virtue of reason, all that the all-merciful Lord will forgive, before Whom all our excuses are corrupt. I, being much sinful myself, forgive and absolve you in the name of the Lord. I suggest to you in advance in such circumstance to consider that when you notice that your weakness is natural, arising from dealing with visitors or from bodily debility, signaled by a smaller appetite, sleeplessness, and such, then it is beneficial to give your body a break, so as not to damage your health being stressed beyond your strength. Then leave the bowing, read half the rule or less according to your strength in the evening, and remain in peace. Do not marvel at hearing a knocking; this is an attempt to put fear in you, pay no heed to it, knowing that the devil is entirely in God's power and does only what God allows him to do for our benefit. Whoever has been in spiritual battle and has not heard the hammering through pipes and the enemy's weapons? Hearing this the brave warrior rejoices, knowing that both the battle and the end of battle are near. A certain girl I know was walking on a lonely road not far from our monastery; crossing a bridge, suddenly a bandit with huge whiskers jumps out from under the bridge and points a pistol to her chest, yelling, "I will kill you!" The girl bares her chest and replies "if this is the will of God,—kill me." Hardly had she pronounced her words than the terrible creature disappeared. I write this to you, so you take courage and use God's terror to defeat demonic terror. With us in the monastery, whoever experiences a fearful event, comes and talks about it, and the source of the frightful event is destroyed by the grace of God, which defends all who are humble, because the humble novice eagerly opens up his thoughts. The fact that you hold your intake breath skillfully, as explained in the *Philokalia*, is well done. The art of this practice is described in a wonderfully brief way by St Nil Sorsky: "Do not breathe quickly, breathing slowly contributes to better focus of the mind." Be satisfied with this: that is, breathe calmly during prayer. When you feel tenderness and love of one's neighbor, all without exception seem like angels. These are the fruits of truthful and unfeigned prayer. And the occasional encounters with temptation, depression, and dreams serve to prove how beneficial prayer is for us. I commend you to God's grace: it will guide you, strengthen you, and lead you, "for without Me you can do nothing" (John 15:5), said the Lord. And again, turn aside from the art of breathing through the nose! When the time comes and God permits this, I will tell you. Once considered beneficial, this art has irreparably hurt some people. Firmness of intention, lack of dreaminess, feelings of tenderness, love for one's neighbors are indicators of true prayer.[43]

∽ Temptations ∽

If we had no one to reproach us, to insult and persecute us, we would never have come to love our enemies. This is required of us by the Gospels, being the highest commandment among them all, given us regarding love of our neighbors. From here we enter upon purity of the heart, through which God appears and by which He is loved. This commandment is as fruitful as it is difficult to acquire. Pray to our Lord Jesus, and He will send grace-filled emotion and reason into your heart as weapons of His justice, through which you will be able to love your enemies and those who hurt you. For, He, as the Son of God, shed His blood for us, his enemies foreseeing in addition that after this redemption, very few of us will be willing to follow His all-holy will.

Regarding the temptations that come your way presently, and those that may come in future, do not pay any particular heed, but do take care to bear temptations with patience and gratitude, praying for those who offend you and calling for their prayers. Do not fear temptations: the same God, Who allows them, He also preserves us through them. We need to develop a sympathy for our temptations and a strong feeling, because through them we acquire the image of Christ's Cross on our souls, through them we are protected from vices. Through temptations we preserve our virtues and only through them are we given grace. Do not justify yourself too much in front of the sisters—because the Lord is Truth Itself and the Veritable Truth, standing before Jewish hierarchs and Pilot, He did not hide the truth, in order not to give them cause for error, but having spoken [the truth] in a few words, He did not justify Himself further, but tolerated slander and suffering in silence, giving us an example how to reject untruth and how to carry the Lord's cross, that is tribulations, sent to us by Him.

I wish that you have love for our Lord God, a most lively love. Also for your neighbors, a love equal to our love of the image of God. May the Lord enable you to see His image in each of your near ones. Saint Mark the Ascetic said: "When one man learns from the words and deeds of another man, the grace of God benefits both men" (chapter 74, *The Philokalia*). This you should also espouse and not allow your heart to entertain human love too much, because many who failed to guard themselves fell away from the love of God. The Right Reverend Philaret, Metropolitan of Kiev, a pastor anointed by grace, told me the following noteworthy words: "Those teachers are commendable who lead their pupils not to themselves, but to God." May the mercy of God protect you.[44]

～ Repentance ～

Instead of my personal word and conversation, accept my sincere written word in which my soul lies open. The defeat of one soldier is not the vanquishing of all the troops. Similarly your verbal sin is not the demise of your soul. These daily and hourly downfalls should not cause immense mourning: for it is a trick of the enemy, who wishes to use excessive sadness to introduce debilitating paralysis to your soul. St Seraphim of Sarov speaks about such sins, and you must not accuse yourself, when such a stumbling block comes your way. Do not think that this is anything new, or extraordinary, we all walk before God with a contrite spirit, mindful of our repentance. This God does not despise: a contrite heart and humble repentance rise above the stumbling block and how many people can be above these hurdles. Amen.[45]

～ Sorrows ～

Whoever does not take up his cross, and comes after the Lord, cannot be his disciple. Taking up one's cross is a sign of recognition that one is worthy of the sorrows you are sent.[46]

～ Struggles ～

It pleases the Lord, and is salvific, to find yourself among struggles which you tolerate without murmur and complaint, knowing your own sinfulness, worthy of eternal punishment, replaced by the mercy of God through temporary punishment. He who rejected a correct or incorrect punishment also rejected his own salvation said St John of the Ladder. Besides, it is necessary to believe that God does not send temptations greater than our ability to cope with them: that is why, before being sent temptations we should bend our neck in humility. May carnal and spiritual jealousy be banished from your society, and may passionless love for the Lord be planted in your heart, and may your prayers pour forth before the Lord for those who mistreat you, for the healing of your souls. Elder Basilisk once heard during prayer a voice: "May you have one goal in your heart during your whole life, to carry the Lord Jesus Christ in your heart and with this you will accept defamation." The Lord himself, all Apostles, all saints spent their life in manifold afflictions. We cannot be saved without defamation. [47]

∼ Sorrows ∼

Do not struggle over the temptation that befell you, but give yourself up to the will of God that saves all who are able to be saved through a variety of sorrows. The mental confusion which befell D was allowed by God for her benefit and her spirit will be saved. Leave her to God. Regarding everything she said and did during her fit, pay no attention and take nothing said or done by her to heart because everything committed by her was outside the realm of reason. That is why such patients are separated from relatives and those close to their hearts, because a mentally insane person needs to be guided by cold reason and a cold heart, which relatives are not capable of handling because they have a close relationship to the patient. When K lived near us during his mental breakdown, his relations were allowed to visit him for a while; after each visit he became worse because they tried to reason with him and soften his behavior. The doctor from the insane asylum told me of the actions of the relatives: "Strange people! They want to reason with the sick man, while his illness consists of his inability to use healthy reason." K would grab a knife, intending to pierce his wife and himself, speaking great displeasure against his wife, while in a reasonable state he regarded her with the greatest care. This is how we need to view those who are ill in this manner. I recommended that P.A. not see his sister until she becomes well. I have a letter from D, from September 24th, from which one can understand the reason for her illness.

You should also not be embarrassed by the words and actions of D during her madness, drawing conclusions from her behavior and not from scientific evidence, which looks very differently upon this illness and its effects. If God permits D to become well then she will be in a good relations with you once more. The fact that she vilified you during her madness is a sure sign that she is devoted to you. You must not grieve about those who used D's behavior against you as an excuse to form an unfavorable opinion of you. This comes from ignorance and is allowed by God's Providence, apparently, to help you achieve humility and a pure heart through the actions of human slander. Have love and peace with everyone including those who offend you, without which one cannot achieve spiritual improvement. Praise God for all that has happened and devote yourself to the will of God. [48]

∼ Temptations ∼

The journey of the Christian, said the Holy Fathers, is to experience one's cross every day guided by the words of our Lord Jesus Christ Himself, Who commanded those who seek perfection to take up their own cross and follow Him. The Cross means one's willingness to benevolently endure any struggle sent to us by the Providence of God. That is why it is said by St Isaac that when a man is constantly beset by struggles he is under a special Providence of God. Drink up slander any hour of the day like living water, said John of the Ladder; whoever rejected a correct or incorrect reprimand has also rejected salvation. The Lord remembers you by sending you temptations for your purification and mortification of the world, all for your own good. I, an accursed sinner, am well pleased with temptations which befell you. Your guardian Angels are also well pleased with your temptation seeing in it your salvation. Remember me, a sinner, in your prayers!

St Isaac the Syrian says that before a person experiences temptations, he prays to God as to a stranger and having experienced temptation prays to Him as to someone close, as if he is now in God's debt. Pray for me to God, servant of God! Because I have not experienced a single temptation in my life and whatever repugnant happened to my heart, it was a trifle, a trifle, a trifle . . ., not deserving any attention, and if I thought to speak of my temptations, then I would only sink into empty chatter. You must not allow fearfulness to take hold of you. Whoever gives in to this passion, him will it rule, and lead you to being frightened by trivia. Read in the holy Ladder the essay about fears. No exorcist prayers are necessary. They were read over each of you during your Baptism. You need to submit to the will of God and consider yourself deserving of any human and demonic guidance. Then fears will disappear on their own. Nothing chases them away like deep and heartfelt contrition.

Do not abandon practicing the Jesus Prayer: all monastics, including those who took vows while being tonsured, also gave their word to practice this prayer day and night.

Look into yourself, try to see your many sins, and in consequence the sins of your neighbors will become smaller. Pursue an attentive life: God has given you this out of mercy for you so you could cry about your sins. When you pray, remember those who offended you, and you will be healed from the terrible affliction of enmity to your neighbor. Remember the ailing D in your prayers, who has been given over by God's Providence to Satan, so that her spirit may be saved. She has contributed to your peace of mind and on the last occasion has contributed to your humility and well-being. In spiritual terms this punishment by God does not serve as a poor estimation of the man:

many great saints were subjected to this kind of submission to Satan: the venerable Cassian writes about the venerable Moses the Black, with whom he discussed the concept that Moses submitted to insanity and possession in consequence of being disobedient to his spiritual father Makarii the Great of Egypt. In another holy composition of the fourth century it is written that a certain Egyptian elder, by virtue of his holy and pure life, was remarkably full of the gift of miracle-working, and his fame spread far and wide. Having noticed in himself the beginnings of pride, the elder began to pray to God, to let him suffer through demonic possession and the Lord answered his prayer. The elder spent the next eight months in a terrible state, even using for food his own excrement. His worldly admirers, seeing him in this position, as can be expected, were tempted to change their good opinion of the elder to a poor one. The elder in good time, rid himself of the demon who possessed him, continued to work in anonymity and peace for the Lord, and came to a much greater state of grace. Madness is of much lesser consequence to the soul than assuming a hostile mental attitude, which is capable of destroying a soul for ages. The fact that D is devoted to you is beyond any doubt.

Pay no attention to her words and actions while she is in mental distress, and you must not compare an insane person with a drunkard, who lose only their ability to reason temporarily but not their mind. A drunkard will spill his secret feelings and emotions, while the insane or possessed person blathers wild thoughts that are foreign to him. If D will get well, accept her without a shadow of a doubt. Thus you will fulfill the commandment of God to love thy neighbor; and people in your monastery, tempted by the words and actions of the insane person, will understand that she insulted you while out of her mind and is being healed and brought back to reason.

We must take unpleasantnesses as precious medicine against our ambition and high-mindedness. The vine which brings fruit, the Gardener covers with manure, in order to bring more fruit. Do not be defeated by evil, rather defeat evil with good.[49]

⤳ Pride ⤳

I look at the stream of my past life, I see a chain of sins, a succession of spiritual falls; almost at every step I was laughed at and abused by the devil for my shortage of spiritual wisdom, for the excesses of my pride, for not inclining to ask advice of my neighbor. My soul is in such a position, and my journey already stretched past half of its designated days. Besides that my body is weakened, pierced, and crossed by various ailments. They are messengers; they tell me of the approaching separation of soul and body. Soon, soon, I will lie on the funeral bed, not for the purpose of giving my overworked body temporary rest but in order to fold it within the ark of the coffin, into the bowels of the earth, from which it was taken, until the future universal resurrection. Remember me Lord, in Thy Kingdom: for my soul is beset by ulcers, and my body is marked by sin. In this state it is more seemly to leave everything and give oneself up to inconsolable crying; when all is lost, one should at least not lose the opportunity for repentance.

But to achieve this condition, which I admit is the most proper thing to do, I use no means except my feeble prayers, in which I ask that the Lord's will be done over me. This petition for the will of God is instilled in me by the fear that I do not ask for something which will exceed my own strength. This fear comes from experience itself: for during all incidents with which my strength was tested, my weakness was revealed; where demons painted before my eyes visions of brilliant achievements, there, in fact, is where I was brought to disaster, there the fatal abyss was hidden by flowers. I learned deception by committing deception; I learned delusion by being seduced and corrupted by it. Now I fear to initiate something special through my own will, even though I believe it to be edifying for the soul. It is better, said the Holy Fathers, to struggle with excrement, that is with fornication and gluttony, rather than with one's own wit, high-mindedness, pride, and superior self-interest. For these last passions are subtle as they imperceptibly creep into your mind, taking the form of sound and righteous thoughts. They cannot be detected except by the light of grace.

I stand before the Providence of God with my mind, setting aside for a minute, the reasoning and wisdom of this world. God created me without my wishing and asking for it: for "nothing" could I wish for, even less to ask for anything. God redeemed the one who was fallen and lost; the price of redemption was God Himself. The Redeemer, clothed in humility, yet clearly God, cannot be recognized as such by carnal minds, who stopped being amazed at kindred spiritual things and chased after alien corrupt things. To me the accursed one, He allowed self-knowledge. When my eyes were dimmed by wax and clay, He applied spittle from His mouth and healed them. The Cross of Christ opens the mind's eyes; the Cross of Christ preserves sanity, heals the ailments of these eyes. Outside the Cross of Christ there is no truth. The World and its truth will be lost because they are from the devil. I stand before my Lord and His Providence and see, and wonder at His long patience, for He is merciful to those who fell into error, who fell into self-will and pride. My soul I hand into the hand of God; whatever He gives me I will receive. He knows my strength, because he gave it to me. If He gives me one talent in accordance to my strength, I do not seek five, in order not to succumb under the weight of them; so the gift, given to serve as a benefit, not serve to become my greater accusation. From my sinful fall I run not into a shelter, not into the desert, but into self-reproach, to the confession of my sins, to repentance. My bewilderment, and my limited ability to reason, and my will I entrust to the endless largesse of Divine Providence.

Such a vision rises before my soul, when I see with the aid of the light of Gospel teaching and not with my own mind. Now I address the words of reproof, found in your letter. The very nature of your observations show that, in spite of my outward behavior, you saw much fewer of my faults than actually exist. Being aware of the greater debt, I cannot fail to confess to the smaller, so I then admit to what I would not wish to admit. It remains for me to tearfully ask your forgiveness and ask your holy prayers for my correction. According to the words of St Isaac, verbal justification does not belong in a Christian life and is not found anywhere in Christ's teaching; if the Lord

Himself, standing before the authority of this world, gave evidence through the universal truth of the Cross and did not deem it necessary to recognize any superficial Truth, not a single word, as dust and ashes, then who, looking deep into his heart, and seeing nothing false, would dare to become one who reproves? Such a one, seeing a sword raised against him, should say: strike, because not in vain is it raised. To disasters, he says: attack and depress me, because I deserve it. To the body, haggard with disease and sent into exile, he says: go, for you have sinned. He will say to his brethren, pray for wretched me, Angels of God. He will fall at the feet of adulterers and murderers, and say to them, pray for me, for You are more righteous than I. That is my condition, when the eyes of my mind are open; when they are closed, then my condition becomes immeasurably worse: for the ulcers naturally remain the same, but disease of the heart is added to blindness of the mind.

From blindness comes insensitivity, loss of love for one's neighbor, loss of tenderness and consoling tears, adding ulcers to ulcers and disease to disease. In other words, whether I see or am blind, my condition is most poor, worthy of tears and crying by all who know and love me. Such is my answer to all who reprove me and you as well. If I answer otherwise I sin. I should have been satisfied with this answer, if I conversed not with my spiritual son, who told these reproofs to me, brought by his heart, did not consider them decisive truths but brought them to me as an indictment. That is why I consider it my duty to continue my discussion, and despite the fact that I am weak, borrowing Light from Veritable Light, the Word of God, to satisfy according to my strength the demands that your letter made upon me, addressing not so much the superficial aspects of thoughts in this letter, but using the light of the Gospel teaching to reveal those mysterious probings of the heart of which these thoughts are the product. In the opinion of the Fathers, those people who demand of their loved ones complete elimination of faults have a false notion on this subject. This view of the Fathers we also find among the Apostles: one of them (John Evangelist) says: "If we say that we have no sin, we deceive ourselves, and the truth is not in us" (1 John 1:8). And the other (the Apostle Paul): "Bear one another's burdens and so fulfill the law of Christ" (Gal 6:2).

What gives rise to reproaches of infirmities in our loved ones was shown in Holy Scriptures among men of the highest righteous character. Who is more saintly than the Apostles? However, we read in the Acts that a dispute arose between Barnabas and Paul that then led to strife and from there to separation. Without a doubt this circumstance was told us in Holy Scripture with the purpose that we, in our weakness, be careful and not entertain imaginary jealousies but carry each other's burdens. And so fulfill the law of Christ! Carry thus my infirmities; and I will try to carry yours, as I have tried heretofore. You will not say, of course, that you have no weaknesses. My weaknesses are harder for you than for me; and your burdens are more palpable for you than for me. If hardships were without burdens, then carrying them would cost nothing, there would be no reason to command otherwise. But the price of mutual carrying of burdens is so great that Holy Scriptures include in this task the completion of the commandment of Christ, who bore the sins of the whole world Himself.

I will say a few words about fickleness. Fickleness, or changeability, according to the Holy Fathers, is the constant, essential frailty of man, as long as he is found in the country of his exile from Paradise on Earth. Steadfastness is a typical condition of future life. Inconstancy is not just typical of us, the weak, but the greatest of Saints also acknowledged it in themselves. Tolerate inconstancy in me and I will tolerate it in you. My inconstancy is felt by you and yours by me. Let us mutually carry each other's burdens and we will learn how beneficial is the yoke of Christ: if we throw off the yoke of Christ, then whose yoke shall we obey? St Elijah Ekdik[50] said it quite splendidly: "The home of the soul is patience, which lives there; and the food of the soul is humility which feeds there." Quite right; thoughts of humble-wisdom maintain the soul in patience. If this is so, then what follows next is also just: nothing else drives patience out of the soul as does prideful thinking, I told you repeatedly and to many others to whom I imagined to impart beneficial knowledge: when I compare my testament with the writings of the Fathers, then I find, had I been among ancient monastics I should have been among the novices. And in today's monasticism, knowledge of Holy Fathers and their thinking is sorely lacking, and teaching about the Holy Fathers is very rare. It is under these conditions that I supervise you as my spiritual children, in order to teach you the Gospel way of thinking, which is the prototype of thought among the Holy Fathers. Truly, truly I say to you: in our time ascetic labor is lacking and spiritual wisdom sorely so. The devil hates this wisdom so much that he would want to wipe it off the face of the earth, because the Gospel is all that remains among us for our judgment. It is not for our edification, for we will be judged according to our knowledge of the Gospel, as the Lord Jesus Christ foretold (John 12:48[51]).

The devil is ready to give us tenfold common sense and a thousand-fold of practical information, just to steal from us the knowledge of the Cross, through which we can stand at the right hand of God. He who appropriates to himself information and common sense likens himself to the devil, who wishes to become the source of light. He is the source of imaginary light: human sophistry, which does not submit to the mind of God, bears the stamp of pride and is the carrier of all conditions of the Fall. "Have you seen one who has fallen? You have seen how you will follow in their footsteps," says Father Dorotheus. This saint spoke about himself that he would rather sin in some outward matter, following the advice of a loved one, rather than to act from self-will. I myself, during any setback, have the consolation of knowing from some small experiments that my work was not done willfully.

Therefore, according to my own unworthiness it is befitting I should heed my own shortcomings; however, according to my duties as an abbot and spiritual father I must say what my sinful eyes tell me: your inner battle comes from passionate pride. Your acknowledgment of practical information and reasoning is how your pride is concealed. Your cooling toward me and those around me are the products of pride: your contempt for your neighbor is followed by loss of love. Loss of love is symptomatic of demonic thinking, just as the acceptance of seeds of grace is denotive of love for one's neighbor. Prideful passion behaves differently from lustful passion, or angry passion. These two passions act obviously and through their justifications and deceptive excuses they are clearer. But pride creeps in imperceptibly. It is sown through opportunity, pomp, and human boastfulness. Although, apparently, we do not accept praise and disagree internally with those who praise us, an invisible imprint remains on our mind and heart, and when we experience humiliation, then we feel pain, and the more pain, the more we feed upon our praise. In this way we prove the existence of the seals and mysteries of universal pride. Alas! The most grace-filled talents were the reason for people to take pride and reap the fruit of their fall! The main symptoms of pride are cooling off toward our neighbors and abandonment of confession. For this reason, whichever doors you enter into, with these doors you also exit, said saint John of the Ladder. Make it a rule to confess your thinking, at least twice a week and since your body conforms to your soul, then express your humility with the bending of your body. Say and repeat your thinking about your brothers: "These are the sheep of Christ, these are the Angels of God" and your condescension toward them will disappear, that is your pride. Then, trusting in the mercy of God, peace and love will enter your heart and grace-filled actions will reveal themselves to you that you are being tempted; your eyes will open and reveal to you your real seduction. This occasion will enter into the treasury of your spiritual exercises, will arm you with precaution for the future; you will gain time for taking nourishment with your brothers. For the man who is not tempted is not skilled and being tempted may assist others, say the Scriptures. May the Lord enable you to follow this instruction from the holy John of the Ladder (Step 4: 6–7): "When once we have entered the arena of piety and obedience, we must no longer judge our good manager in any way at all, even though we may perhaps see in him some slight failings, since he is only human. Otherwise, by sitting in judgment we shall get no profit from our subjection."

It is absolutely indispensable for those of us who wish to retain undoubting faith in our superiors to write their good deeds indelibly in our hearts and constantly remember them, so that when the demons sow among us lack of faith in them, we may be able to silence them by what is preserved in our memory. For the more faith flourishes in the heart, the greater does the body grow in service. But he who has stumbled on distrust has already fallen.

Care for our neighbors sometimes leads to pride, just as a corn-cockle[52] at times grows from the wheat kernel. Therefore, St Mark the Ascetic said: "When a person uses the words or deeds of another person, then both benefit from the grace of God." "For we do not preach ourselves," says the deposed Paul, "but Christ Jesus the Lord" (2 Cor 4:5). Whoever will cultivate these feelings, in him the passion for people will dissipate and love of Christ will reign, in all who see the image of God. When the mind becomes delighted with this consoling love, then man sees himself as a vessel filled with stench and filth and marvels how the rays of Divine teaching shine through him and heal the human soul.

It is proper for me to recall here the words of St John of the Ladder repeated by Nil Sorsky: "Some sank in the swamp, but others were guarded from a similar fate and for that the Lord granted them salvation." For after experiencing serious spiritual ulcers I learned that evidence of pride is found in disparagement or scorn of one's neighbors and negligence of confession, while pride itself is not noticed by the man, being a refined passion which brought down a light-bearing Angel from Heaven. This passion is the cornerstone of other passions, just as buildings whose foundations are hidden underground.[53]

∽ Trials ∽

Illuminated by the word of God we confess that temporary struggles are a great gift of God. These are given to chosen servants of God, who are being prepared for eternal bliss, and that is why we greet you and those beloved of our Lord with the words of the apostle: "My brethren count it all joy, when you fall into various trials" (Jas 1:2). The venerable Mark the Ascetic advises that when afflictions happen to not see the One, from and through whom struggles occur, but rather seek to endure them with thanksgiving. St John of the Ladder said: whoever rejects any prohibitions whether they are right or wrong also rejects his own salvation. Similarly the Holy Fathers reason that the man of faith believes that God rules the destinies of all persons and receives each temptation as his own: for God's rule cannot be mistaken or unjust. Look well inside yourself and you shall see what is bewildering you. You are confused about human justice, which is more like demonic justice, whose purpose is to cause you to renounce the Cross. Say in justification to yourself: "Get behind Me, Satan! You are an offense to Me, for you are not mindful of the things of God, but the things of men" (Matt 16:23). I follow Christ on the Cross and through slander, ridicule, in short, through all unpleasant and difficult things, I accept as my own, as a gift from God, sent to me through His mercy. Amen. [54]

∿ Sorrows ∿

I'm sorry about the sorrow that has befallen you! You already know that struggles need to be endured, in the hope of receiving God's mercy and His help. By placing all hope on the Lord our God, the ascetic of Christ must attempt to remove the reasons for the affliction, if it is within his power. Such diligence is appropriate for you as well. I sincerely wish you patience and spiritual prosperity. If circumstances do not permit me to see you in this earthly life, my memory of you will remain intact in my soul, and I earnestly wish to help you with my wretched advice in the Lord, when my help is required.

May the merciful Lord forgive you all your sins and may He strengthen you against all temptations.[55]

∿ Repentance ∿

Inasmuch as I am writing to a servant of God and for the sake of God, then I will leave all worldly reasoning, in order not to be distracted by one or other human impulse and not to become a traitor to your soul, which came to me for advice about the Lord, and has reason to accuse me before the Lord at His Last Judgment, should I in this vain world damage my counsel through hypocrisy, flattery, or human want. I believe according to the heritage of the Church and with the Church that every Orthodox believer in Christ who keeps His commandments, and when he violates them cleanses himself through repentance, will be saved. That is what the Lord himself told the young man who asked how he could be saved. However, there is another purpose for Christianity, for which monks are appointed in particular and that goal is sometimes achieved and sometimes not: Christian perfection. The road to this perfection is through cleansing oneself with the commandments of the New Testament, with the Gospel, by which the son of the Old Adam may be guided in order to be adopted by the New Adam. "And everyone who has this hope in him," says St John the Evangelist, "purifies himself, just as He is pure" (1 John 3:3). But the new testament is "exceedingly broad!" The new commandment reads: "For whoever desires to save his life will lose it" (Matt 16:25). What does it mean to lose one's life? It means rejecting one's own impulses and constraining oneself to act in accordance with the commandments of the Gospel. The Gospel communicates to one who acts this way, its own mind and its own sensations, which belong to the nature of the new man, regenerated accordingly to the likeness of Our Creator and Our Redeemer. This involves coercing and forcing oneself as prescribed by the Gospel. This means the advice, so often repeated by the Holy Fathers: "Give blood and receive the Holy Spirit." Cut off attributes of your fallen nature and graft to yourself the properties of the new nature generated by Christ.

Not only our "flesh" but also our "blood" will not inherit the Kingdom of God. Just as "the Kingdom of God is within us," so we must conclude from this that until movements of our heart are accompanied by movements of our blood, then spiritual actions, emitting from God, are also absent. By virtue of spiritual Divine actions blood calms down and creates a "mighty silence." That sacred world is not present in our fallen state, rather it is given and gifted by the Lord: a world more elevated than any mind descends into the soul. It pours forth a divine stillness into the mind, heart, and body of the servant of Christ, unites these three into one, and presents them to Christ, submerging them into profound humility, bringing us in the presence of Christ. This condition belongs to renewed nature. Having been invited by you to give you advice beneficial to your soul, advice about the Lord, I turn attention away from my own stinking sores of the soul and address you, I tell you for the sake of God and with a heartfelt cry the following: you demonstrate a natural bodily fire and your blood is alive. For this reason there is no room in your heart for Divine fire, which the Lord came to plunge into us and which extinguishes our own natural fire. "When you have both (fire and blood) . . . says St. John of the Ladder . . . you are misled." You have movements which actually are dependent on your blood; they block the emergence of the movements of the Holy Spirit, keeping your soul in darkness, in some kind of undetermined state, felt by you but not understood by you. It is not understood because such movements can communicate only opinions about knowledge but not knowledge itself, which is clear, precise like truth. Because of this, when you view yourself and enter into yourself, your conscience responds to you vaguely, with a terrible voice of conceit. You are in need of consolation: may you be comforted by the Truth!

Let us look at two aspects of what we are now discussing: about love for our neighbor and the action of mental prayer.

You are alive for people. You love them with a natural fire. That is why people are alive for you, and Christ is dead. (Do not be embarrassed by my words: in my words, above, I made a distinction between salvation and perfection, ceasing to discuss the former, for the sake of God's certain mercy to you, I am now talking about the latter, about purification.) In the second part of the *Philokalia*, in the book by monks Kallistos and Ignatius, in the 37th chapter are the following words of the Great Barsanuphius: "If you are not possessed by people in the world, you will dwell in the city," and if you die to every human, then you shall inherit both the new Jerusalem and treasure in Heaven. Do not fear this kind of death; from it a new life is born. When you come alive to this new world, then you will see that this life on earth, whose end is demanded of us by God, is death. This is that death, for which Adam died immediately upon tasting of the forbidden fruit, having revived in that mixed sensation of the knowledge of good and evil. Tell God about all your relatives alive and passed away, about the brothers of your monastery, about all those you love: "Lord! All this is Yours, and who am I?" Exactly, all this belongs to God; all that is God's we will not steal for ourselves. And what we allegedly love should better belong to God than to us. Is that not so? If that is true, then let us accept truth for our salvation. Let us die to the natural love of our neighbor and come alive to Him, the love of God. Then we shall die a natural, mingled death to our neighbor when we do not impute ourselves, according to the advice of the Great Barsanuphius: with all men, "when we spit upon ourselves, as a kind of abomination. Let us serve our neighbor in our service, not like fathers to their children but as slaves to their Lords, as useless servants of the Holy Angels." That is what Paul wanted also and how he reasoned! "For we do not preach ourselves, but Christ Jesus the Lord, and ourselves your bondservants for Jesus' sake" (2 Cor 4:5). Let us give what is God's to God. Our opinion will not usurp what is God's and make it our own, and we will only deceive ourselves with empty delusions deserving both laughter and tears. When we humble ourselves, then God may give us what is His; only then it will become ours through grace. Thus the Saints became vessels of the Holy Spirit and had spiritual children. The commandment of God, "Do not call anyone father, nor teacher on earth," remains unchanged. When Ananias and Sapphira lied before the Apostle Peter, they then fell dead, as the apostle explained their fault that they lied to God, even though they stood not before God but before a person, the apostle. But this person was the vessel of the Holy Spirit; whatever was done against him was done to God. Many among the saints called those people children, to whom they communicated the life of the Holy Spirit. And that was true, because words were accompanied by the very action. But can we, not having a clear presence of the Holy Spirit in us, appropriate to ourselves that which only God can give? Isn't this terrible sacrilege? Is not this self-delusion that produces a false condition, deserving of bitter crying? Those Holy Fathers, who did not shed abundant grace, like the Apostles and other great saints of God, did not dare to call themselves teachers and fathers. Of these the venerable Nil Sorsky spoke in the preface to the Skete Rule: "Do not call yourselves my students: there is but One Teacher among us, Christ" etc. And this by the will of the apostle, who says: "If anyone speaks, let him speak as the oracles of God. If anyone ministers, let him do it as with the ability which God supplies, that in all things God may be glorified through Jesus Christ" (1 Pet 4:11). Everywhere the word "I" is mortified! Everywhere Christ lives and gives life. Humility destroys natural (physical) love. If natural love dies from humility, then her life consisted of pride. Belonging to the properties of ancient Adam, natural love needs to be mortified and regenerated by the Holy Spirit. The idolatrous "I" lives in natural love, placed there on a throne stealthily through conceit, hidden by a curtain of supposed virtue.

The Apostle Paul did not care for this love of his disciples for him; because of this he called them carnal. Arming himself against this, he wrote against himself, wishing to diminish, drop, and eliminate himself in the opinion of his disciples. "Was Paul crucified for you?" (1 Cor 1:13) he said to them. "Who then is Paul? . . . I planted, Apollos watered, but God gave the increase. So then neither he who plants is anything, nor he who waters, but God who gives the increase" (1 Cor 3:5–7). You see how zealously the apostle urges that believers in Christ be deadened to mankind! Coming alive to men means being dead in relation to Christ and consequently toward all things Divine and spiritual: that is why Christ is the only mediator between God and men.[56]

The disciples of John the Baptist became envious, having learned that all are following on the trail of Jesus, and the great Forerunner answered them: "He who has the bride is the bridegroom; but the friend of the bridegroom, who stands and hears him, rejoices greatly because of the bridegroom's voice. Therefore, this joy of mine is fulfilled. He must increase, while I must decrease" (John 3:29–30). Great words! Holy words! Exactly then do disciples fulfill their duties when they seek to find those they bring to Christ that He alone is exalted and growing in their souls. They wish to diminish themselves in the opinion of those they lead, in order to magnify Christ in them, then these disciples feel the fullness of joy having reached the end of their desires. On the other hand, those who bring entrusted souls to themselves, and not to Christ, I say unfailingly, they commit adultery.

Now, with God's help, some words about mental prayer! During your practice, you can experience actions directly from your blood and an inexperienced practitioner can take that as grace-given, as it reads in the fourth part of the *Philokalia*, in the piece by His Holiness Patriarch Kallistos of Constantinople with the title "The example of focus in prayer." One can find in the actions, arising from the blood carnal feelings, a certain sweetness and imagine that this is the product of prayerful delight. Such thinking is self-deception, called by the Fathers "Conceit." About this "Conceit" St John Karpathos says, at the end of chapter 49, that this is satiety of the soul (rapture of the soul pleased with itself, pleased with an imaginary state of sweetness) and the opinion of "vanity of mind" that comes from such contentment or satiety. The Apostle Paul writes to those who found themselves in this state of self-delusion, called "conceit": "Behold those who are sated, those who have become well-off, those who have tasted sweetness." If they really became wealthy, why the reproof? If the apostle reproves them, then it means they only had a conceit of wealth. "Conceit does not suffer one to be imaginary," says St Simeon the New Theologian. This may be the conceit of prayer, obstructing one from gaining knowledge and tasting the true effect of prayer.

The Most Holy Lady, our Theotokos, and Ever Virgin Mary spoke about those who think highly of themselves, saying: "He has filled the hungry with good things, and the rich He has sent away empty" (Luke 1:53). "There are those with nothing that make themselves rich," says Scripture, "and there are those, though very rich, who humble themselves" (Prov 13:7). How can the poor become rich? Through conceit. But their fate deserves pity: while the hungry will receive blessings, they depart empty-handed. And in the next life "but from him who does not have, even what he has will be taken away" (Matt 25:29). Can imaginary wealth be real? Having been reproved and denied at God's Final Judgment the very same conceit, what will those who had this conceit be left with? With empty hands.

What can be said about the actions you felt during prayer? They are decidedly originating with your blood. You cannot fail to recognize that your thoughts are also at work. Your conscience, suspecting the validity and accuracy of these actions, and doubting them, can already act to reprove these actions. In addition, you are in the dark. Divine action would have illumined and satisfied you, not through feelings of sweetness but with the knowledge of Truth, from which appear in the conscience a wonderful calm and a confirmation. Warmth travels over the surface of your body, but you have absolutely no knowledge (this comes only with experience) how your soul moves in harmony with your mind; draws the body with it; how does a person moving in a fine cool mist in the midst of the vast world, connected to himself, overcome all battles, distance himself from all sin, clothe himself in repentance, stand before the face of the Lord with a pure prayer that embraces all his being, even the very clay and spittle he is made of. Only then your blood calms down, imaginary sweetness departs, the person sees that he is a fallen creature, is guided by repentance which must embrace him, make it possible for him to be purified, and through purification experience union with God. Repentance must be the soul of prayer, without which prayer is dead, stinking with the stench of proud and seductive conceit! Repentance is the only door through which one can obtain from our Lord the saving pasture. He who neglects repentance is bereft of all grace.

Your blood is alive, but your soul is dead. To enliven the soul one needs the Spirit. Adam was created with a living soul, that is the Spirit of God coexisted in his soul and brought it into motion; that is why this action was a spiritual action, in God. After Adam sinned through disobedience, the Spirit of God stepped away from Adam: Adam's soul died immediately, and his flesh and blood came alive. By these means through flesh and blood the devil began acting upon the soul, kept her in the dark, in a state of death and captivity. That is why one needs to mortify not only the flesh but the blood also: if the blood is not mortified, then in spite of the silence of bodily passions, the devil can still hold the soul in captivity by action of its passions. If the soul does not become pure and propitiate God with repentance, there are no other means through which it can feel spiritual actions. If the soul does not come alive (movement is a sure sign of life), then seeing and knowing the passions of the soul are not possible. And if one cannot see the bonds that bind us, how can one become free of them? Finding oneself in these bonds, the soul is in the realm of the devil, who keeps her in darkness and lifelessness.

You ask: "What movement of the soul?" "The carnal mind and the carnal heart . . . cannot be ascended by the soul." I reply: repentance is needed so that the soul is capable of such a movement: let it bring you the knowledge of this divine movement. There is no other way to know this movement except through experience; words are ineffective at expressing this: it does not belong to the corrupt physical world. Believe, enter into repentance with simplicity, and "the Divine will come to you of His own accord," as Isaac the Syrian said. God is faithful: to those who knock, He opens; to those who cry, he consoles, to those who are poor in spirit, he bestows the Kingdom of Heaven. Do not think that repentance is easy: this is the heart of all struggles, this is the complete struggle that should animate all other struggles. Those who remained in true repentance achieved genuine results. This is the major struggle, which prepares us for the acquisition of the Kingdom of Heaven. The Saviour Himself announced this! "Repent," He said, "the Kingdom of Heaven is at hand" (Matt 4:17). The merciful Lord prepared the way for our divine heavenly, eternal Kingdom, showed the door through which we might enter into the salvific pasture of the Holy Spirit and Truth, the door of repentance. If we neglect to repent, without any doubt, we will remain outside of the door. Good deeds, natural in feeling, will in no way replace repentance. St Simeon the New Theologian counted the good deeds received by him from his mentor, Simeon the Pious, of whom he said "he taught me penance!" No matter how you count, it is not through good deeds alone by which you achieve eternal, unutterable treasures. Through repentance is found the whole mystery of salvation. How simple this is, how clear! And yet how do we behave? We abandon what was indicated to us by God, salvific repentance, and seek to exercise imaginary virtues, because it pleases our senses, and little by little, inconspicuously, we become infected by self-conceit and since grace is in no hurry to crown and reward us, we compose for ourselves sweet sensations, which by themselves reward and comfort us.

Is this not funny? Is this not stupid? Is this not proud and arrogant? Let us stop fooling with God (forgive me this impolite expression, which I did not hesitate to use because by this means exactly our behavior is characterized!). Let us live before Him in constant repentance. The time is coming when the Final Judgment is being prepared for us, which will judge us not by our conceits, by which we flattered ourselves, but by the Truth. Let us prevent the frightening eternal disaster through repentance, avert the eternal cry with our temporary crying. Come to your senses, sinners! The eleventh hour already struck and the opportunity to struggle in our field will soon, soon end. But, there is still time to judge yourself, in order not to be judged by God. Hitherto we have justified ourselves.

The beautiful turn of phrase of your letters reminds me of the letters of Barsanuphius the Great. Your expressions are lively, aflame, and strong. Such is the superficial appearance, but if one judges from a spiritual point of view, then one must say something else. The letters of Barsanuphius the Great are quickened by the Spirit; all things human are mortified, and the Holy Spirit alone is alive. Your letters are alive with carnal blood and passionate fire; in them you are alive, and people are alive—God is not present!

You were pleased to write: "a brotherly, friendly, trembling care about one who needs help, I did not find" (that is you in my letters) etc. This is the direct movement of action in you animated by the person. Why mention trembling in your letters, if it is not the result of movement of the blood?

Let me continue (quoting what you write): "Would not you like to see your good student and follower clothed in the Holy Spirit, our brother" etc. Here is an example of a person animated by both self-deception and pomp.

I brought these citations to you as examples, but on the whole, everything is marinating in one and the same marinade, that of ancient Adam. Understand, that we, as people of the Fall, possess a mixed consciousness and the knowledge of good and evil, acquired through the sinful fall of Adam. Christ destroys this mixed condition through the Gospel, replacing complex knowledge and feelings with simpler sensations. But how can we as the fallen and lost not be used to delights, even natural ones, by virtue of our damaged nature (even a delightful drink is forbidden, into which is dropped just a tiny amount of poison!); we are given by our Saviour a common and ceaseless task, the practice of precious repentance. It is invested by our merciful Lord with a short and humble consolation, which eases our conscience, gives us hope of salvation, which is called by the Holy Fathers "the good news." What an appropriate delight for sinners! How great and wise is the Lord's mercy!

For one who remains on the road of repentance with faith and constancy, the ineffably gracious Lord increases consolation, tenderness, and a sensation of insignificance of the person. His chosen ones and most faithful servants are henceforth imprinted by the Holy Spirit and once in a while are given a Taste of the life to come. Certainly from time to time they become participants in inexpressible spiritual consolation. On the other hand, anyone who creates delights for himself, that one is clearly in demonic delusion![57]

∼ Repentance ∼

My heart speaks more than what words can express. And strange! No sooner does my heart wish to start a discussion with you than it

flows into a prayerful state and takes me into that darkness, which acts
to bring us close to God, the light for His intelligent creatures. Carry
yourself there also! It is good to forget the man in God, because God
remembers him. It is good for you to be dead to the man in God; this
is true life, life in the Spirit. The Spirit mortifies and gives life. He who
comprehends, let him understand, and he who is unworthy will find
the spiritual word is hidden in the light of the world that is inaccessible
to the carnal mind.

Take a look: despite man's limitations, how much he devised,
he made many things to satisfy the manifold needs and whims of
his! Incomparably more remarkable is the Wisdom of the all-wise
and all-powerful God seen in the countless reasoning creatures
He created. Each human vessel carries a separate, unique, and dis-
tinct ability! Each human vessel is a container with its own unique,
spiritual gifts. One is capable of service, performed by the body;
another is capable of acts of mercy; a third is capable of prayer and
silence; another is able to shepherd the souls with words of Truth and
Spirit; another has abilities to lead people and find a place for them;
another has the gift of providing society what they need for temporary life here on earth: food, clothing, homes, and the like. Your
vessel is for the sacraments of the Spirit. The Spirit of God is Holy,
residing only in the pure and saintly. Purify yourself with Truth,
not of the human, foolish kind but Divine Truth. This descended
upon humankind from heaven and was preserved for men in the
Holy Gospel. It says: "Learn from Me for I am gentle and lowly in
heart, and you will find rest for your souls" (Matt 11:29). That rest is
the place of the Holy Spirit: At "Salem," says Holy Scripture, "is His
place" (Ps 75:3).

The property of Divine Truth is to purify, to release. The Lord said:
"If you abide in My word, you are My disciples indeed. And you shall
know the truth, and the truth shall make you free" (John 8:31–32). He
prayed to the Father for His disciples: "Bless them" (that is sanctify
them with the Holy Spirit) "in Truth." "Sanctify them by Your truth.
Your word is truth" (John 17:17). And to His disciples He said: "You are

already clean because of the word which I have spoken to you" (John 15:3). Therefore, those wishing to comprehend truth, to be purified and freed by it, must study with their mind and deeds the commandments of the Gospel, even if it must be accompanied by coercion of the heart, laden with corrupt, sinful [antagonistic to God] inclinations and passions. In the commandments is the Truth; in the commandments is humility; in the commandments is love; in the commandments is the Holy Spirit. All this is confirmed by the Scriptures. "All Thy commandments are true" (Ps 118:86), sang the God-inspired David: "He who has My commandments and keeps them it is he who loves Me" (John 14: 21). "Abide in My love. If you keep My commandments, you will abide in My love" (John 15:9–10). "The words that I speak to you are spirit, and they are life" (John 6:63). To the one who is corrected, pre-purified, comes the Holy Spirit, as the Spirit of Truth, suddenly, incomprehensibly enters into the mind, body, and soul, refreshes him, and makes him born again into life in the spirit. "I opened my mouth and sighed, because I was longing for Thy commandments" (Ps 118:131). May the Gospel commandments be the subject of your study, reflection, and your activity the rest of your life. "Abide in Me, and I in you" (John 15:4) through the observance of the Gospel commandments, said the Lord,—you shall "bear much fruit" (John 15:5). On the contrary, "without Me, you can do nothing" (John 15:5), that is no spiritual virtues. Virtues common to every fallen human nature are like nothing, have no value before God, and are destined to hellfire. "If anyone does not abide in Me" by following the Gospel commandments, "he is cast out as a branch and is withered; and they gather them and throw them into the fire, and they are burned" (John 15:6), regardless of any virtues of his fallen nature.

In your prayers, plunge entirely into repentance. There is a condition of being reborn, you know it; and you are in a state of disrepair! Therefore, continue your incessant, salvific cry. Deny yourself! Nor should you count your life dear to yourself (Acts 20:24) by example of the holy apostle. Consider yourself only among the condemned. Be selfless before God. Under no circumstances allow yourself to expect grace: this is a condition and teaching among those who are under delusion, those who have fallen away from Truth. Seek to see your own sin and mourn over it: that is your business. And God will do what He will, because He is faithful, and gave His promise, and will fulfill it. The Grace is His!

To give it is His business. Do not consider your garments pure, and worthy of the temple of a bridegroom, no matter how much you have Washed them: your judge is God. I liked how you served your parent. Let the Reason for your service be not your blood ties but the commandment of God, which said: Honor your father and your mother that it may be well with you, and your days may be long upon the good land the Lord your God is giving you (Ex 20:12). Everywhere replace the flesh and blood with Christ. He will remove you from earth and lift you up to Himself in Heaven. I am copying certain sayings from the Holy Fathers: "A monastic Brother asked the great Sisoes: 'How can I be saved, how can I please God?' And the elder replied to him: 'If you wish to please God separate yourself from the world. Leave creation, come to the Creator, interact with God by means of prayer and crying, and you shall find peace in this and the future world.'" The great Barsanuphius said: "if you stop caring for all things material, then this will bring you closer to the city. If you do not involve yourself with people this will help to place you in the city. And if you mortify yourself [separate yourself from all humankind], then you inherit the city and all treasures therein."

A brother asked Abba Pimen: "What shall I do about the passions embarrassing me? The elder replied: let us cry before God's blessedness, until God deals with us according to His mercy."

"Another brother asked the same great Pimen: 'What shall I do with my sins?' The elder replied: 'he who wishes to cleanse himself from the sins he committed, and protect himself from new sins, will be cleansed with his cries. This is the way of repentance, inherited by us from Scriptures and the Fathers, who said: cry, because there is no other way except crying.' The great Pimen said: the beginning of anger is distractedness."

"He also said: If you will be silent, you will find peace everywhere, no matter where you live."

"John of the Ladder wrote: he who tires out the body, but keeps his words to a minimum—is humble, entirely the home of love." "He also wrote: close the door of the cell for your body, the door of your tongue for speech, and close your inner door against the spirits of deceit." The following is taken from the forty-first word of St Isaac the Syrian, briefly:

> Most of all love silence, because it will bring you close to the harvest. Words are insufficient to express it. At first encourage yourself into silence; then from silence something will be born inside you, which will enable you to be silent. Then God will allow you to feel something born from silence. If you begin living this life, who knows how much light will shine upon you from this. Do not imagine, that the silence acquired by the wonderous Arseny was the result of his own natural character. No! At first he coerced himself into silence. In this manner of life there is born in us a quantity of tears and wonderful sights. Great is the man, who carries in his soul the habit of silence. Silence assists in wordlessness. Those of us, living among others, are unable to avoid meeting people: even the equal to the angels Arseny, who grew to love silence above everything else, could not distance himself from meeting others. It is impossible not to meet those we share living quarters with—our Fathers and brothers— accidentally, going to church, and during other events. Realizing this, the worthy man taught himself, instructed by grace, to perpetual silence.

In his twentieth word St Isaac teaches the monk to speak to his soul thus: "You lived your life like a madman, in lewdness worthy of any punishment. At least preserve yourself this day, from the days remaining to you, spent for nothing, short on good deeds, rich with works of evil. You came into the world mysteriously and reckoned to die for

the sake of Christ; do not come alive again for the sake of the world
and for all things that belong to the world. If you anticipate peace,
you shall be alive in Christ. Prepare yourself for every form of vilification, for every chagrin, every shame and reproach from all quarters.
Accept it all with joy exactly as you earned it. Endure with gratitude to
God every illness, struggle, and sorrow from demons, whose will you
committed. Endure every need and natural grief! Endure with trust
in God the bodily deprivations which shortly turn into pus. Incline
your neck to all this, hope in God, not awaiting from anyone else any
consolation, but focus all your care upon the Lord and judge yourself
the only cause of all these troubles. Do not be tempted by anything, do
not blame anyone for the insults you endured, because you bit into the
fruit of the forbidden tree and gained a variety of passions. Accept all
the bitter medicine with joy: may they shake you up a bit and you shall
find a sweet reward. Alas! Alas to your stinking vanity! Your soul, full
of sins, you left unattended, as if it was not subject to any accusation,
and were busy judging others, whom you judged with your words and
thoughts."

Theophil, Patriarch of Alexandria, having visited the practitioners
of silence on mount Nitreian, asked their Abbot, a Great saint of God:
"What did you find especially important in the monastic life?" The
spirit-bearing Abbot replied: "to blame oneself and reproach oneself
constantly."

The Venerable Pimen the Great called self-reproach that anchor,
which held the spiritual boat tied down during a storm. Here are
examples and evidence of feats, already familiar to you, which can
bring your soul abundant profit and give you enduring spiritual education. Do not think that for learning of silence you need a closed cell
or a far-off monastery. No! It is much better to learn among people
with the help of spiritual struggle. Your very falls, invisible to your
neighbor, shall be seen and known to God and your conscience will
serve to benefit you, making you skillful at dealing with sin, revealing to you all the weaknesses of the human condition. The ascetic,
brought up among people with the aid of the invisible inner struggle,

will be durable, rich in knowledge and spiritual experience, full of humility, and for his neighbor. He shall be a haven, a treasure. He will be like the tree, grown on an open hilltop, subject to rough winds and all kinds of inclement weather; such trees grow deep roots into the ground, are especially juicy, full of life and strength. On the contrary, the sapling grown under the protective and solitary life of a monastery is like a flower or tree, brought up in the shelter of a greenhouse. He is used to a fatal softness: any small storm and he suffers; some stronger weather and he dies. Complete solitude, according to the rules of spiritual life, is allowed only for those, whose ascetic struggle, as expressed by St John of the Ladder, was blessed by the descent of blessed dew from the Holy Spirit. For such a one it is beneficial, necessary to have a strict seclusion, in order to assist them to submit fully to the teaching and direction of the Spirit, about which it is not time to speak now.

If I am not worthy to be called a person, having in me much that is beastly and demonic, then you, by your love for me, ascribe to me the dignity of man, or at least, the dignity of a reasonable creature, even though marked by the sorrowful fall of Adam and Eve. The Son of God calls himself in the Gospel Son of Man; God, appeared among men, did not take upon Himself any imaginary fallen human title, calls Himself a name, given Him by God, which before creating us, consulted with Himself mysteriously: "Let us make man" (Gen 1:26). Son of Man! How I like that name! What a wonderful name! A humble and sublime name! How didactic and comforting it sounds in my ears! People did not want such a name, they need: Your Reverence! Your Excellency! What nonsense! And their behavior echoes the names, became senseless, an ugly caricature, in which pride is joined to foolishness. On the envelope, I permit you to write whatever nonsense you wish, but in the letter, be man to man, like heart to heart, before the eyes of the all-holy God. May your heart converse with me simply, sincerely; let each of your words be for the truth. And God! As He is, may He be a witness to our conversation, whose reason and goal is He and our salvation is in Him.[58]

∿ Detachment ∿

I received your first letter of September 7th. Much has been written in answer to it in my letter of the 5th. That is why I put to myself: to wait with the reply and then reply to your two letters at once—all that God would insert into my unworthy heart and have at my command one arm that hardly writes from weakness. I am constantly sick and frail, especially in winters, but now in addition I take medicine, which heals the pains but takes away my strength. I was thinking to write certain details about spiritual exercises that suit you. I am stopping to fulfill this to another time; am hurrying, having received your second letter, to help as best I can, with God's help, to restore the peace of mind that has been disturbed. And you ask me to hurry with the reply.

"Go quickly!" said the Lord to Moses, heeding His Mysteries in solitude, on top of Mount Sinai, in the seclusion of darkness, brought upon by the clouds which descended on the mount: "Get down from here! For your people, whom you brought out of the land of Egypt, are transgressing the law. They turned aside quickly from the way I commanded them. They made themselves calf, and are worshipping and sacrificing to it" (Ex 32, 7–8). Know that when a man finds himself outside peace, he is in an erroneous condition in relation to the law of Christ, in a state of delusion and self-deception, in service to idols. I gaze at the waves churning in you—and there is no sadness in my heart; they do not frighten my heart, do not bring any doubts. My heart is calm; furthermore it feels a spiritual consolation. What is the reason for this? My heart is sensitive by nature; it cannot be cold and indifferent. I can tell you this: my heart sees with conviction that you have the mercy of God. Such a determination about you came from the elevated altar of the King of Kings. Do not fear storms, do not weaken from them: they are a good sign. You will soon be overshadowed with God's help; the scale of your heart shall receive a heavy spiritual treasure, from which all your earthly cares will be outweighed by a cup without weight. Believe my heart! I do not know if it is worth trusting, but it assures me so strongly that I, leaving behind all reasoning and mental exercise, write what my heart commands me. I see a spiritual harbor prepared for you by the all-merciful God, waiting for you. But He, the all-merciful and all-wise, at first allows you to work with these waves, to tire you out, to struggle in your fight with the waves, and give value to the harbor. Man does not give adequate value to something that is given him at too cheap a price. Was not the harbor paradise? And that harbor was not given much value by man, he was unhappy with it. He wanted more, he wanted the impossible!

Forgive my lack of modesty, which allows me to encourage you: I am ineffably embraced by the spiritual, educational consolation, which is overwhelmed by the sweetness of my mind, which collaborates with inspiration coming from my heart. "Now, O Israel, listen to the ordinances and judgments I teach you today to observe, that you may live and become numerous and inherit the land the Lord God of your fathers is giving you," said the Lawmaker of Israel, the God-seer (Deut 4:1). One who is tested by many waves writes to you, by the many cliffs and underwater rocks. Yet I am still not thoroughly tested by the many tribulations that stem from as early time as I can remember. Much have I suffered! Suffered more from my fiery blood, from my fiery love for my neighbor, love, conjoined, it seems, with pure, complete sacrifice: from an inclination for justice and honor from my carnal mind. Now I must heed and watch my own blood; without this watchfulness, it will plunder holy peace from my heart, without watchfulness, the blood will remove me from mentorship by the Holy Spirit and deliver me into being led by Satan.

Know that God rules the world; He has no unrighteousness. But His truth is different from human righteousness. God rejected human truth, because it is characterized by sin, lawlessness, and the fall from paradise. God established His all-holy truth, the truth of the Cross, which opens Heaven to us. It pleases Him that we enter the Kingdom of Heaven through many tribulations (Acts 14:22). God gave in Himself [in Christ] the image of the realization of this: He, having become incarnate in one of His worshipful hypostases, submitted Himself to a variety of insults and humiliations. His most Holy Face was subjected to beatings about the ears and spitting. He did not turn His Face away from this. He was counted among the lawless; counted among them, he was sentenced to a humiliating, common penalty, submitted to it by what kind of people? Nefarious villains and hypocrites. We are all without answers before this supreme Truth; either we must follow it, or these words will apply to us: "And he who does not take his cross and follow after Me is not worthy of Me." "He who is not with Me is against Me" (Matt 10:38; 12:30).

Against the truth of Christ, which is His Cross, rises the corrupt truth of our nature. Our flesh and blood rebel against the Cross. The Cross calls the flesh to be crucified, demands the shedding of blood; and the flesh seeks to preserve itself, to reign, to take pleasure. The road to the cross is all about struggles, vilification, deprivation; men do not want to take this road; they are proud, they want to flourish, and be eulogized. Do you understand that flesh and blood are prideful? Take a look at decorated flesh and abundant blood—see their pomp and ostentation! Not without reason are we commanded to experience poverty and fasting!

I wrote you that as a witness of the deeds and teachings of the Holy Fathers, he who wishes to move from a carnal existence into a spiritual one must be mortified before all men. What kind of a death is there without illness! During our meeting I told you: "You must be alone, solitary." Your heart and mind realized the justice of what was said, but your blood heard your death sentence upon it and was horrified. I understood this and did not hesitate nor do I hesitate to tell you the truth, necessary for your salvation and your spiritual prosperity. Hear, hear the voice of a sinner, the word of a sinner, chosen by God as a weapon for your coming alive to the Spirit, and even though it requires the shedding of bloody sweat, fulfill this. With your sword and your bow take the Earth away from the Amorites,[59] give it to the Son of the beloved Father, to the mysterious Joseph, to Christ. So did the pre-figuring figure of the holy Patriarch Jacob ["Moreover I have given to you one portion above your brothers; I am giving you Shechem, which I took from the hand of the Amorites with my sword and bow"] (Gen 48:22). The Earth, I call your heart; the Amorites your blood, flesh, evil spirits, who rule this Earth. You must retake the Earth with the help of ascetic struggle, that is with prayer of the mind. How and with what can we heal your sickly attitude? Do you believe in the Saviour? Do you believe His words? He said: "But the very hairs of your head are all numbered" (Matt 10:30), so watchful and caring down to the minutest detail is the Providence about us by our all-blessed God, who cares so much about us and accounts for every hair on our head. He sees the First-martyr Stephen being beaten by stones and does not prevent the murder. He sees the Apostles dying daily, suffering ceaselessly, and ending their earthly journey with a violent death. He sees thousands upon thousands of martyrs undergo amputation, sawing in two, breaking of bones, long confinement in stinking and stuffy dungeons, deadly work in mine shafts, burning at stakes, freezing in a lake, drowning in water. He watches the monks commit invisible martyrdom in their battle with the flesh and blood, with unclean spirits, with people who love the world, with countless deprivations of the body and the spirit. All this He observes, the Lover of mankind, and the Almighty. From all this He could have saved His chosen ones, but He does not do that, informing us His servants: "By your patience possess your souls" (Luke 21:19). "But he who endures to the end shall be saved" (Matt 24:13). "But if anyone draws back, My soul has no pleasure in him" (Heb 10:38).

The sons of Zebedee asked the Lord for thrones of glory and He gave them "His cup." The Cup of Christ is a gift of Christ, given by Him to those He loves, to His chosen. The Cup of Christ is a condition, which secures eternal bliss. The Cup of Christ is suffering. St Isaac the Syrian wrote: "Therefore it is known as a special Providence of God over man, when that person is sent endless sorrows." In conclusion I will cite the words of the Apostle Peter: "Let those who suffer according to the will of God commit their souls to Him in doing good, as to a faithful Creator" (1 Pet 4:19).

Based on everything said above, I say that N is under a special Providence of God; everything happening to him is all before the eyes of God, with God's allowance, his Creator, Saviour, and Lord. . . . You really have not seen God in His Providence and in His governance? Reverently depart you insignificant speck of dust! Stop the hand that dares to reach with the hand of God for the reins of the destiny of man! . . . Stop yourself! Sober up your mind, intoxicated with gusts and waves of blood: your ailing heart presented God to you, abandon the reins, which belong to Him alone, having forgotten Your most sacred promise.

Proceed with the healing of your leprous and flaccid, raging soul. Relying on faith, on living faith, get up every day: at first several times a day, three or four times for a brief moment on your knees, and say to the Lord: "Lord! N, whom I thought to love so much, to respect, deceiving myself I called him my own. But He is Yours, Your creation, Your very own. He is Yours, all-blessed Creator and Lord of all! You are all-blessed: You wish to arrange all good things for him. You are all-powerful: You can arrange everything, whatever you shall wish. You are all-wise: Thy ways of the spirit, Thy spiritual destinies, humankind cannot investigate or conceive. And who am I? A speck of dust, a handful of earth, existing today, gone tomorrow. What benefit can I bring him? I can only hurt him and myself more with my impulses, which are carnal and sinful. I submit him to Your will and power! He now is and always was in Your full will and power; but I did not see that through my blind mind. I give You back your property, which I pilfered like a madman from You, flattered by my own self-delusion and imagination. Heal my heart, which thought to love, but which only hurt—because it loved outside of your holy commandments, in violation of the holy world, in violation of the love of You and my neighbors." And we are commanded to love our enemies; and a violation of love to them is an infringement of the commandments, a breach of love for our neighbor. Arising from your knees, repeat several times unhurriedly: "Lord! I submit him and myself to Your holy Will; may Your will be done in all things! For everything, glory to You!" When you are among people, and you see that unseen temptations arise in your soul, repeat the words just written above. When you see confusion in your world, in your little world of the monastery, repeat these words: "Lord! You, are all-powerful, see everything; may Your will be done, may your inconceivable destinies be accomplished. And what am I but a speck of dust that should not intervene in your inconceivable governance."

The Son of God said of Himself: "The Son of Man is being betrayed into the hands of sinners" (Matt 26:45). If He, the all-holy, is delivered into these hands, what is strange about a sinner being delivered into the hands of sinners like himself? Let us learn to speak like the sinner crucified next to Christ "I shall receive according to my deeds; remember me, O Lord, in Thy Kingdom."

And N should conduct himself similarly, regarding you. He should submit you to God and His will and providence. For spiritual leadership he is weak, being drawn to your weakness. And in your weakness there is a great power of the blood, eloquent blood, which stands up against the rule of law: those who have not realized in themselves clear spiritual action that gives freedom, independence, they cannot stand up to the force of your blood. "You must be alone." I repeat this to you: those who seek battle with you will be injured and perhaps incurably so. My lot was constant solitude; it was and is. What to do? Endure the burden of solitude. Seeing it, seeing us as orphans on this earth, the Holy Spirit, in his own good time, known only to Him, will come to us. Then you will not be alone and will take joy in the fact that you were alone. Mortify your mutual passions with true humility, which is offered in the above-mentioned prayers to see God.

When you encounter thoughts of jealousy and tenderness to N, and he to you, say to yourself: "Lord, he is Yours! And what am I?" When the struggle intensifies go immediately to your cell and fall on your knees! Striving thus you will feel the grace of God, which heals you from the addiction to each other, by which you are deprived of your individual freedom; you are in captivity and suffer thus. Your time and health are lost in empty confusion and fruitless suffering. When God gives you healing from these passions and you feel the freedom and ease, you will realize that your real condition was "temptation," it was a false condition, not a spiritual one, and that is why it was sinful, abhorrent to God. Small things which go unnoticed while living in the world become enlarged in a monastery setting and become important drawbacks, capable of causing incurable harm. They can not only stop but end all spiritual growth, making life in the monastery completely fruitless. This applies especially to monastics, who have labored in Christ's field and realized some progress in internal prayer and other internal ascetic struggles.

Certain short words in the above-mentioned prayers and humble words must be rotated more frequently before the face of the soul, in order that a variety of insects not have time to land on the soul and make it sore. They belong among the strongest and effective arms for one's invisible spiritual battles. The use of these and similar arms is an ascetic work of internal prayer that is the foundation of the walls of spiritual Jerusalem, by which the walls built by the enemy in our hearts come tumbling down. "You must be alone!" "Become as good as dead to others." May they fall on the edge of the sword of the Levites, those faithful to God, their brothers and neighbors, worshippers of idols. Thoughts and feelings that are the servants of God must cut off the thoughts and feelings of the soul that are servants of sin. Their parents are one and the same: the mind and heart; that is why they are brothers. They are close and neighbors: that is why they look close to kindness and are very attached to the heart. When, by orders of Moses, the sons of Levi girded their swords on their thighs and went about the camp of Israel from gate to gate, killing each relative and his neighbor, then Moses said to them: "You filled your hands to the Lord today, each one on his son or his brother, that blessing be given to you" (Ex 32:29). And you should act thus that a blessing may be given you. If you will not be good as dead to people, if you will allow your heart to be involved with empty attachments, your entire life you will creep upon earth, incapable of anything spiritual: your bones will be deposited outside the Promised Land.

Do not fear any struggle or battle nor giants! Like a true Levite do not spare any brothers, sons or daughters, relatives or neighbors! Do not be moved by pity for your blood, which kills with eternal death which condescends to your kin! Go for the sword, Leonid, for the sword! Into battle, desperate battle! Fight the persistent battle, an enduring one, until you win the crown of decisive victory! "Better to die during struggle, said St. Isaac, than to live in corruption [the fall]." And what kind of a life is it that is lived in sin? It is not worthy of the name life; Holy Scripture calls it death; it is the beginning of eternal death, maybe even death eternal, if you do not mortify yourself for Christ. How many frail elders, gentle maidens, or weak children remained victors? Will you really allow your divided soul to shake you, to drop from your hands the victorious crown of eternal joy for the price of momentary, suffering vacillations, which circumstances, mockingly, abusingly present to us as virtues. Do not fear the strongholds of sinful halls: with perseverance "strengthen your attack against the city," says Scripture, "and overthrow it" (2 Kings 11:25). Yes, I will see the crown of glory on you, the crown of the Spirit, at first on your head, and then your heart! May living water flow from their sources! And from these sources you shall drink, first, until you are satisfied. Then others who are thirsty for the Word of God will drink from these and praise the Lord. Spiritual love of your neighbors will reward you a hundredfold for your extermination of that love that stems only from your blood. Before your renewal be alone before you compound any special love for someone. I speak about spiritual relations that are a kind of fornication. After your rebirth there appears a true love of neighbor, holy, spiritual: it is all about God; it is a spiritual vision. It is worth shedding blood for when you are rewarded with the immense treasure of the Spirit. By acquiring the Spirit a man sees clearly that blood is ungodly stinking filth. And that is why Scripture says: "Cursed is the man who does the work of the Lord carelessly, keeping back his sword from blood" (Jer 31:10 LXX). Die! Die! And be buried in order to inherit the holy resurrection of your soul with the Spirit of God.

Just as you should not communicate your struggles and spiritual temptations to others, so you should not listen to theirs. The private reason for this: your blood is strong and hot. You convey yourself strongly and receive in the same manner. That is why you stun others with your perturbations and become offended at struggles heard from them. The other reason is found in the general rule for all ascetic strugglers: spiritual warfare is not possible to grasp and explain by natural reason, because all our nature is in a corrupt state. For that we need a spiritual mind, that is one that come to a man from the action of the Spirit. That is why only a man who has spiritual training can listen to the ascetic struggles of a neighbor and offer him salvific counsel. One who is still in the grip of dark passions is not capable of this. Be silent, be silent! First you need to be silent, according to the advice of the holy Psalmist, about the benefits themselves; then you must not rebuke your mouth, when the teachings of your mind, that is the constant flow of thoughts, begin to flow with Divine fire.

You write: "To abandon N is to throw Christ Himself in his face, naked, wounded, and tied to the prisoner's post? Will He not abandon me as well then? You see how eloquent your blood is? Who would not be swayed by it! You, like Cicero, are capable of begging mercy from Caesar for the most hated Appio Milon . . . just as Demosthenes raised all of Greece against Phillippi. Have mercy on the weak! Do not overwhelm them with your strong language! Spare also the afflicted, who vividly feel and suffer for others more powerfully than they themselves!" Into your charming expressions there have crept what the Holy monastics call "excuses." Justification is the mask of virtue with which the catcher of souls covers his nets that he has spread about to seize our mind and heart. We pray on our knees to rid ourselves of justifications: "Incline not my heart unto evil words, to imagine excuses for sins with men who work wickedness" (Ps 140:4 LXX). St Pimen the Great spoke about our natural, fallen will and about our justifications:

"Our human will is a copper wall between man and God, a stone cast in battle. If a man abandons his will, then he will say: 'And by my God . . . I shall leap over a wall . . . It is God . . . made my way perfect'" (Ps 17:30, 33 LXX). And when the will is joined with justification, then the man dies. Your "very own will" is the inclination of your heart toward N; your justifications assist your biases; you think, you speak, invisibly Divinely, and you suffer terribly. You could, if you do not take action, damage yourself irreparably. For your simplicity and sincerity God sends you a helping hand! Do you understand that your heart is of the simplest kind? There is nothing complex about it. You are useless to the world: the world needs cunning ones. You can be cunning and secretive only when you are silent. Get accustomed to silence: it is necessary for you, and you must remove spiritual heroism and external, fruitless sorrows. Your needs to be devoted to God! Your heart to the Holy Spirit: He likes to rest in the hearts of the simple and gentle. You are gentle but your blood trips you up. Overcome your blood with humility and silence. Look more often upon Christ: "This is My Son," witnesses the Father about Him. "Behold! My Servant whom I have chosen, My Beloved in whom My soul is well pleased! I will put My Spirit upon Him, and He will declare justice to the Gentiles. He will not quarrel nor cry out, nor will anyone hear His voice in the streets. A bruised reed He will not break, and smoking flax He will not quench, till He sends forth justice to victory; and in His name Gentiles will trust" (Matt 12:18–21). Never argue with your thoughts. The enemy may use logic, unfailingly, to incline our mind to accept crafty, suicidal thought, disguised in a mask of virtue and piety. The test of your thought process shall be your heart. No matter how attractive is your thought, if it deprives you of "peace" in your heart, and craftily disturbs your "love of neighbor," this thought is your enemy. Do not argue with it, do not reason; or it will catch you and move you to bite the forbidden fruit; arm yourself quickly against it and chase it away having armed yourself spiritually: "Glorifying God," "Thanking God," "Surrendering yourself to His will," "Accusing and blaming yourself," "by praying." Excellent arms suited for powerful battle: go to your cell,

turn yourself toward God for a moment asking for His help and submit yourself to His will. In intense battle this scene is repeated several
times a day and it helps a great deal.

Have you been observing your mind? Have you studied its attributes? Your mind is not analytical, which parses all things piecemeal,
dissecting them; and after such labor comes to a conclusion. Most
human minds have analytical qualities, and that is why they are able to
be cunning, to cleverly arrange their affairs and intrigues. Your mind
sees and embraces things without much labor. Your mind is made for
spiritual vision. Notice another thing about your mind: it is capable of
freely and joyfully falling in the dust before the majesty of the Divine,
but in order to be reconciled with your neighbor you need to work
on yourself. Why? Because by nature, your mind has contempt for all
things vulgar, vile, and petty; it is incapable of bending and twisting.
Seeing these shortcomings in his neighbor, your mind has contempt
for both the neighbor and his shortcomings. Your mind is directed by
the Gospels and will then be reconciled to each neighbor when he sees
Christ in every one.

All who have been baptized into Christ are clothed in Christ. No
matter how or what they did to defile themselves, the robe of Christ,
before the Final Judgment, is always upon them. It is necessary to
consider oneself the worst of all men: this requires holy humility. The
apostle did not simply say that he was the chief among sinners; he was
convinced of it. And we must persuade ourselves: this requires hard
labor. May the Lord give you and me this commitment. By virtue of the
nature of your mind, because of its unique character, distinguishing
it from other minds, you will have to carry and are probably already
carrying certain sorrows. Rarely will you be understood. Seeing your
mind's sharpness and glibness, few would believe that your mind is
simple! Most people will consider you cunning, clever, and will sus-
pect you of all manner of things. This is unavoidable: analytical minds
cannot imagine the existence of a mind without analysis, looking simply and clearly. Seeing the power of the mind, they will ascribe to it a
high degree of ability to analyze, expecting a deep, refined capacity for

cunning in everything you do, while you look with perceptive simplicity on everything, with the eyes of men. Forgive your neighbors. We are all weak. To follow the law of Christ consists in our ability to carry each other's burdens with equanimity, grace, and humility.

I am pleased that you have not read many books on religion: it is better to have a blank writing tablet rather than have one that is scribbled over with nonsense. Should I write on yours? If so, then let there not be the lifeless words of people but the life-giving words of the Spirit. Seeing your trust in me, I am assuming the right to send you, as time permits, books on the writing of the Holy Fathers, whichever I shall judge would benefit you. Whatever is "mine," I shall make "yours" and send it to you: that was my habit: I saturated myself exclusively with reading the Holy Fathers of the Eastern Church, carefully stored, according to their own holy advice to keep them apart from false teaching, keeping only those containing the saving grace of the only true Church. Please receive "mine," when God instructed you to desire it. Do not read any foreign compositions: they replaced the Holy Spirit with wild and flaming blood. These books can lure you into an abyss, as they attract many there. The Holy Spirit is not present there; they have their own spirit: a very dark and swarmy spirit of heresy and pride. The "action" you mentioned was formed in you by the Holy Scriptures: such an impression was made upon John the Evangelist and the Myrrh-bearers by the far-off sounds of the hammers, beating upon the nails during the Crucifixion of our Redeemer, this was "bloody." Understand: the nervous system was shattered. Such actions repulse the spiritual struggle and are called "delusions," that is, they arise from the self-deception and affect those who are present, because they are not from the grace of God but from one's own human condition, common to our fallen state, which arises from our strained imagination and emotions. Those inexperienced in spiritual matters ascribe these feelings as grace-inspired; hence comes the opinion of oneself; internalized emotion is self-deception or delusion. That is why we must keep ourselves in a state of coolness, calm, quiet, humble in spirit, removing oneself thoroughly from all conditions which lead to the heating of the blood and nervous system. Do not slap yourself on the chest, nor your head, to expel the tears: tears come from the shock of the nervous system and do not enlighten the mind nor soften the heart. Expect tears which come from your submission to God. Some holy invisible finger, some very fine thought of humility will touch your heart and a quiet tear will come, a pure tear, which will change your soul, without changing your face; your face will not become red, a humble peace will pour into the expression of your face, making it Angel-like.

When I read in your letter the following "not a single ray of grace nor any evidence of kindness did I find in it about how loudly and much people spoke. And Your gentle heart believed my plea and correctly judged my irritability," from the bottom of my soul I laughed. I need your written answer in order to justify myself to myself. I trust no one so little as myself. Who am I, to lead a human soul to God, created in His image and likeness? My soul wanders in the wilderness. It is mired in mud. I must devote time during my earthly pilgrimage to the care of my soul. That is how I see myself with my eyes. Christ be with you.[60]

⌒ Friendship ⌒

In quiet solitude, on the shore of the majestic Volga I remember you often, you blessed couple! And you are on the shore of a sea, which is peaceful at times, clear as a mirror, and yet at other times the surface is troubled by a storm that creates turbid waves with silver foam. Such is our life! Calm and tempest alternate with each other; and time passes, passes, seeking to plunge into the abyss of eternity. Blessed is that swimmer in the sea of life, who often directs his gaze heavenward. By heavenly bodies he charts his path, does not despair during storms, nor does he trust the calm sea: it is so fickle! The eyes through which heaven is visible is our faith; through faith we discern the spiritual heaven: the teachings of Christ. In that heaven the New Testament shines like the sun, the Old Testament like the moon, the writings of the Holy Fathers like the stars.

I write you directly from my heart what it was inspired to tell you. My heart is moved by the same sweet simplicity toward you as you have toward me. Such a relationship is a true treasure. Love for one's neighbor is the greatest delight! And what consoles me especially in my friendship is that the reason for this friendship is God. He, as it says in the Scriptures, enlightens and sanctifies all things; He is the source of all true blessings, of all actual pure delights. He will keep me in your memory and you in mine. He will allow us to redouble our gift of friendship, received from Himself. Here is what I wish: I wish that upon stepping into eternity we be honored among the assembly of the blessed and faithful servants who appear before the Lord and say to Him: "You gave us the fine gift of friendship, we bring You the other, acquired through friendship: a gift of precious salvation."[61]

∼ Friendship ∼

Friends were given me by God: this gift I accepted from His all-blessed right hand in exchange for my offer of selflessness made early in my youth. My own experience proves the truth of the Gospels, which command us to leave all behind, in order to inherit all. The New Testament strips man of that which he governs incorrectly. From this peaceful refuge, from this distant monastery I repeat the same thought I spoke of from the other monastery near you: "Do not get carried away by the noisy, rapidly flowing stream of the world!" May the ears of your hearts attend to my pleading voice!

Christ be with you![62]

∼ The Law of God ∼

May the blessings of God shine upon you newlyweds! A blessing so abundant that you could clearly see it, one that would console you, for which you would thank God. To those He loves, He sends struggles followed by consolations. When struggles are replaced by consolations, and vice versa, they engender faith in God and indifference to the world. Faith, having taken man by the hand, places him before God. Such a person rises above the world: beneath his feet is the dark chaos of doubts, unbelief, misconceptions, pompous, and vain punditry. And at the feet of one who reached the peak of a hill are clouds, elevations, and precipices, the rush of waterfalls skipping over cliffs.

Earthy life is an endless journey, uninterrupted, not even for an hour. Come, come: suddenly the gates of eternity swing open, and we are lost in its visually unimaginable space. How fine are the words of St David: "I am a pilgrim upon earth: O hide not Thy commandments from me" (Ps 118:19). So the law of Christ is a thread by which we are lifted from the dark labyrinth of earthly life into blessed eternity.

∼ Patience ∼

In the deep, dark night the melancholy echoes of the town's criers call out the hours, interrupting the sacred peace of the night. The voice of one crier cheers and comforts his companion: the very thought, or feeling, that there is another person sharing the same fate, the same task, warms his heart.

It is both comforting and gratifying for a Christian to hear the voice of his brother under this dark and deathly canopy in which we proceed on our earthly journey, on our road to heaven. What shall I tell you from this distant post of mine? What comforting thought will the sounds of my words carry in your direction? Hear that which brings me a special benefit: hear the words of the Saviour, offered by Him as a general benefit and edification as a reinforcement for all wanderers on earth: "By your patience possess your souls" (Luke 21:19). Ah! We need to remember this instruction of our Saviour, we must hold onto it ceaselessly, as a blind man holds onto the hand that guides him, because sorrows every now and then, pass over as a wave to a wave. They sell us from one to the other, as a cruel lord sells us as bondsmen from one lord to another lord, each new lord more cruel than the first. Thus when our soul and body have wasted thin with struggles, and grown weak and useless like a spider's web, the grave is ready to accept us! . . .

In order to overcome one struggle, one needs courage; to be released from a second struggle, one needs wisdom; to be delivered from a third, humility is required. But in dealing with all struggles as well as with every virtue, patience is essential. Not a single virtue can be accomplished without patience; it cannot be sustained without it. He who is shaken in his virtue will not endure to the end and even that which was acquired will be lost. The Lord said about those who seek to serve Him that they bring forth fruit through patience (see Luke 8:15), instructed them to acquire their soul through patience (see Luke 21:19), informed them that only those who endure "to the end shall be saved" (Matt 24:13).

Here is my response to your call from my solitary place! May it penetrate the inner chamber of your heart, may it echo inside your heart, may it pour forth therein a tender consolation, a consolation that brings a heavenly word and heavenly hope. This is the voice of one crying in the wilderness, one silent in the desert! . . .

I plunge again into my silence, into my distant place, into my anonymity, dark, inspired, as the deep night. Thus the town crier returns to his silence, having sung out his periodic melancholy call![63]

~ Patience ~

I do not like it when wanderers of the earth are insanely jolly: such a demeanor is not appropriate for exiles, for whom death is waiting, then judgment and a twofold destiny: blessedness or torment. I prefer them to be calm: calmness is a sign that the wanderer has blessed hope in his heart.

I live in solitude where I receive treatments. The action of medicine is lifesaving, but also has a strong effect, as a result of which I must lie down for days on end. From my windows there is a wonderful view of the Volga, for which I give thanks even though I gaze upon it infrequently, rarely, in passing. I remember myself in childhood: I was not receptive to the physical world, the material world had little effect on me. I was not curious but cold to all physical things. But

I could never look upon a person with indifference! I was made to love human souls, to admire the souls of men! For that reason they are before me, so Angelic! They appear before the eyes of my heart so captivatingly, with such comfort! What a spectacle, such a picture, upon which I look, peek, and look again. I just cannot look enough. And so strange! The face, the form, the features I immediately forget, the soul I remember. There are many souls, beautiful souls in my mind's eye, written by love, which my faithful memory preserves in complete integrity, in vivid color. Due to my solitude that coloring becomes even clearer, more bright. You and your brother are in my vision as well. I look at you often! My soul is filled with blessings for you both.

Whether in a luxuriant outfit or in a simple little dress, what difference does it make? Let us complete our wanderings in this life, carrying the lantern of our right and living faith. This lantern will lead us into the eternal Kingdom of God. Before entering this both rags and sumptuous clothes are removed: even the most opulent outfit in comparison to the luminous spiritual garments will be nothing more than a contemptible rag.

"By your patience possess your souls" (Luke 21:19)—it is said to wanderers on this earth, because our journey is narrow and sorrowful, and we are infirm. "My strength is made perfect in weakness" (2 Cor 12:9). Holy Scripture comforts us once again.[64]

∼ Judgment ∼

You must take careful heed of your soul. Do not squander it. This can happen. How many people do so! Remember that you also need to depart from this world by way of the grave's gate, to stand before the judgment of God. The Last Judgment is both for His Saints and for those who spent all their life in blessed service to Him. Not only sins but the truths of men will be judged there; there the many truths of men will be judged by the All-perfect truth. The Saviour himself gave witness to this, saying: "For I say to you, that unless your righteousness exceeds the righteousness of the scribes and Pharisees, you will by no means enter into the kingdom of heaven" (Matt 5:20).[65]

~ Patience ~

Are your wanderings on earth conducted favorably? During his wanderings a person can observe events that happen before his eyes; he may imagine that his journey to eternity has ceased. That is a delusion of the eyes of your soul. We continue walking, never pausing for a minute. For the wanderer on earth who follows the difficult path, an encouraging song is given, lest he lose his way. The melody has these elements: "The Will of God, the sacred Commandments and God's statutes." "Thy statutes have been my songs in the place of my pilgrimage" (Ps 118:54), so said the inspired David. So it is in these parts, when someone is lost in the wood the neighboring villages ring their church bells expecting that hearing this sound the lost party will come out from the dark wood.

A dense, highly populated town has something in common with the vast and deep wood: one can get lost in either. Let my voice coming from my solitary place be like the sound of the blessed church bell: may it always sound in your soul, may it always find shelter there. May your soul hear it now! Having heard the sound of my voice, may you reap true consolation! I think man cannot find true consolation, except by his remembrance of God. Having remembered God, says the saintly David, man shall be exulted.

How true it is that we all must die! That this life compared to eternity is nothing but an insignificant moment! No man has remained immortal on this earth. And yet still we live as if we were immortal; the thought of death and eternity slips away from us, becoming completely foreign to us. This is a clear testament to the fact that mankind is in a state of fall; our souls are united by a kind of gloom, by some kind of indestructible bonds of self-delusion, with which the world and time hold us in captivity, in servitude. We need to constantly exert ourselves, to constantly struggle, to fight with oneself, in order to swim out from this dreadful, dark abyss; we need patience, in order to magnanimously endure all the unseen storms of the soul. Temptations found in our mind and heart are more terrible than any external temptations. No one is as dangerous to us as we are ourselves. "Watch and pray" said the Lord, " lest you enter into temptation. The spirit indeed is willing, but the flesh is weak" (Mark 14:38). To keep watch over oneself is only possible by the light of the New Testament. The light, by which spiritual watchfulness is accomplished, also pours forth from the writing of the Holy Fathers. Holy Scriptures and the Holy Fathers ceaselessly remind us of God, His good works, our purpose, the future which is either eternally blessed or endlessly miserable; they expose the deceit of the world, its intrigues, and show what resources there are to avoid these intrigues and how to enter the harbor of salvation.

Remain a servant of God in the short span of your earthly life and you will inherit eternity filled with joys and unceasing spiritual delights. One must inherit eternity! Do not despair over stumbling blocks, the state of being free of sin is an impossible dream! Stumbling blocks are natural to all mankind, who, due to this very inclination toward falling, are instructed by Christ: "By your patience possess your souls" (Luke 21:19). "But he who endures to the end shall be saved" (Matt 24: 13).[66]

∽ Renewal ∽

We were all united as one through prayer. This bond is higher than all earthly feelings; this is something heavenly; this is a foretaste of future life, in which all men will be united by the Holy Spirit. Here on earth, things of the earth serve to bind humanity. The earth I call our flesh and blood. So said the Lord: "earth you are" said He to fallen man, "and to earth you shall return" (Gen 3:19). After the Liturgy I had the true heartfelt pleasure of bringing you greetings on your saint's day to wish you all blessings, which the merciful Lord will dispense in eternity to all those who please Him and whom He loves. Today I come to you from my place of seclusion by way of my thoughts, remembrances, with my heart, finally, with these lines. I greet you on your saint's day and greet you with the same spiritual joy, replete with the same sincere and blessed wishes for you. May the Lord bless you! So that "thy youth shall be renewed like the eagle's" (Ps 102:5). Through devotion man is renewed and grows younger. If one compares the earthly life of man with eternity, we are all equally young or old. I see only the pious one in all his color and beauty of youth; he is truly alive. He radiates the spiritual sweet-smelling fragrance of immortality; one senses the One who dwells within and animates the man. Thus all can clearly detect the soul in the actions of the body that serves as its tool; the absence of the soul is also felt. All can see this through the inaction and stench of the cold corpse.

There is no greater joy on earth than to experience God and to cleave to Him with all your soul. This union is from now to eternity! It is the condition of true bliss, a bliss that is eternal, whose foretaste already begins here on earth.

When I think of you, I associate the thought contained inseparably in this verse from the Psalms: "thy youth is renewed like the eagle's." And my heart sends you this thought on the wings of a powerful wish!

It pleases God that your soul be open to me for both our benefit. The one who speaks and the one who listens to the word of God both profit, and the one who brings the benefit is God. He unites here on earth people of like mind, in the vale of sorrows and tears through His all-holy, all-powerful word. At the end of their earthy wanderings, He settles those of like mind into their eternal home, where the spiritual feast never ceases. Here on earth he gives us like-minded accord, which is pleasing to Him and unanimity of thought as a pledge; and there, in heaven, in eternity, he gives unspeakable bliss, as a fulfillment of His pledge. What a thought just came to me! I will not hide it! May the merciful Lord allow me to see you with all your children and grandchildren in your eternal home, full of light and happiness, glorifying God completely, as I saw you all last year on the 14th of October, gathered in His holy temple. You created a shelter for God in your home, so do the same in your soul; He will make your home as it were a splendid dwelling in His holy city of Heavenly Jerusalem. He will do so, because he vowed to reward each person according to his deeds.[67]

～ Repentance ～

The Lord said: "No one can come to Me, unless the Father who sent Me draws Him" (John 6:44). Therefore, although the instrument of the calling is man, nonetheless it belongs to God; the one who calls is God. Having heard this call, which became audible to you after you completed many of your wanderings on earth, let not your heart be bitter. It becomes embittered by sinful flattery, as St Paul the apostle said. "Beware, brethren, lest there be in any of you an evil heart of unbelief in departing from the living God" (Heb 3:12).

I do not advise you to go into a detailed and refined examination of your sins and the traits they create. Gather them all into one vessel of repentance and cast them into the abyss of God's mercy. A very fine sorting out of one's sins does not suit a person in the world: it will only lead to despondency, bewilderment, and embarrassment. God knows our sins, and if we will constantly turn to Him in repentance, then He will gradually heal that sin, that is the sinful habits and characteristics of our heart. Sins, which originate in words, deeds, and the sum of our thoughts, need to be confessed to our spiritual father; but a very close examination of our spiritual qualities, I repeat, should not be attempted by the laity: that is a trap set by the catcher of our souls.[68] We can recognize the trap by the effects it has on us, namely embarrassment and despair, even though externally the trap gives the appearance of plausible goodness. This dark cloak is needed by monastics, in order to cover up the rays of grace, which emit from their mind and their heart: by those who have realized a measure of grace, whose vision of their own sinfulness cannot bring them to despair but only drives them further into repentance. Thus the God-seer Moses carried his cloak over his radiant face.[69]

We need to recognize, as can be fully justified, that all of us find ourselves more or less in a state of self-delusion; all of us are deceived, all of us carry this deception within us. This is the product of our fall from Paradise, a consequence of accepting falsehood for the truth; thus we continue to fall even now. This is why we are so fickle! In the morning I am thus, by noon I am changed, after midday someone different still, and so on. Both worlds act upon me, I am subject to both, a prisoner to them. The world of spirits acts through our thought patterns in our hearts; the material world acts through our physical sensations. Both worlds beckon us to taste the forbidden fruit. To our physical sensations, through vision, hearing, and touch, this fruit appears lovely; our thoughts come from the words of an invisible voice, which prompts and insists "taste, discover!" The voice entices us with curiosity, goads us through our vanity. There echoes in our soul the voice of the seducer, the voice first heard by our great-grandparents in Paradise: "and you will be like gods, knowing good and evil" (Gen 3:5). The voice echoes and tempts; tempts and kills. That is why man is given a new virtue: "humility," given a new inner labor: "repentance." Both the inner labor and the virtue are truly strange! They are radically contrary to the reason why we fell. Through repentance we overcome the fatal sensations of our physical state. Through humility we defeat the arrogance, flattery, pride of our life—in short, everything that drives a person insane.

How should we be? We need not be embarrassed by recurring change as something unusual; we must not pick through the details of our sins, but must conduct our life in constant repentance, calling ourselves sinners in all respects. We need to believe that every person admitting his sinfulness will be received into the arms of the merciful Lord, into the center of salvation. Understandably we are not speaking of deadly sins, whose repentance is received by God only when the person stops committing these. Jobs around the house and on the land are very beneficial: they keep us from idleness and assist with the invisible battle being waged inside our mind. The battle with idleness elevates us to a greater struggle, permitted only to those who are brought there by circumstances or by Providence. Prudence demands that we not take up a battle that exceeds our strength: Quite the opposite! Given the opportunity we need to ease our struggles. Believe in the all-powerful God, have hope in Him, live with patience and constancy, live in simplicity, in humility and repentance, dedicate yourself to the will of God, and when you lose your way, direct yourself once again to the right path, and you shall be saved.[70]

∼ Combat ∼

Your last visit to the Sergiev Hermitage is fresh in my mind. I saw you there, when earthly fame, so inconstant and fickle, was smiling at you. Now you seem more majestic to me; you left a deep impression upon me. I respect all virtues, but none inspires such respect in me, as the patient generosity of spirit that accepts changeable fortune here on earth. On the field of battle, a man often becomes a hero when blood boils in him; in the upheavals of life one can be a hero by having a mighty heart. A valiant man, coming down from the heights of military exploits, refashions his sword of special alloy into a plow or scythe: the sword that sounded thunder to enemies of his country; and every true citizen, bolstered by history and his progeny, will gaze upon this plow with reverence; he will join the ranks of great men. Contempt and outrage produce false signs of distinction, which decorate the chest of some scoundrel: on that chest each medal is a memento to some intrigue, something base, some evidence of idleness. Tell me, what of it, if the head of Grishka Otrepiev[71] wore the crown of Monomach? What was the source of his glory? . . . The glory of a dark shameless, unconscionable evildoer, who would not stop at any lawlessness, a glory that is inseparable from curses. May God preserve us from such glory. And how many pretenders there are!

Not everyone can be the leaves, the flowers, and the fruit on the tree of the governing authority; after all, someone needs to take the role of roots and give the tree life and strength by working behind the scenes, anonymously, quietly, fundamentally usefully, performing a necessary service. One of those activities, I admit, is the affirmation of one's neighbors in the Christian faith and morality. This peaceful, humble activity with the living word and pen always absorbed a significant part of my time; and in my ailing state, it would occupy all of my time. Things have not come about according to my wishes, did not result in accord with my assumptions; I assumed that certainly I would be dismissed: there were so many collaborators toward that goal! Instead, I received a temporary leave in the Babaevsky Monastery for my rest and treatment. This is where I now am. Locked up without hope of exit from my cell, doing everything necessary to fight the chill, which penetrated by my body deeply, producing there a nervous weakness, which keeps me largely bed-bound. My future is unknown . . . And I waved my hand at it! . . . I said to Almighty God: "Do with your creature as You wish. I believe in Your word, that not even one hair on my head will fall without Your will."

Oh my soul! Swim fearlessly on the waves of the sea of life, not trusting its stillness, not fearing its storms. Do not consider the next day, do not tire yourself with any assumptions, any dreams, do not spend any of your strength and time on these things. "Sufficient for the day is its own trouble" (Matt 6:34) said your God! . . . Believe! Swim, get carried by the waves! . . . Life on earth is a deception. You will not see how already before you is the harbor of the grave. Where there is faith, there is no sorrow, no fear; there is fortitude and strength, which nothing will defeat.

In his youth, a person is occupied with acquiring knowledge, needed to expand his circle of action in the material world into which he steps as an active member. The skills needed for this are acquiring different languages, knowledge of the fine arts, mathematics and sciences, history, and philosophy. When man begins to incline toward old age, then time draws near for him to shed his outer garment and reveal the fruit within (the peel I call his skin and body, the fruit his soul), as he prepares to step into the measureless sphere of eternity, the region of the spirit, then the object of his study becomes not the changeable material substance, subject to finite destruction, but his object becomes the infinite, indwelling spirit. It matters little how this or that word sounds when all sounds must cease! It matters little what this or that measure is taken when one faces the measureless! It matters little about this or that petty thought, when the mind prepares to leave scattered thinking and enters into an elevated realm of visions and silence, created by an infinite God for creatures of limited capacity. The study of the spirit gives a person a stable character, appropriate for facing eternity. His horizon broadens, his vision reaches beyond the limits of the material world and time, from which he brings an other-worldly firmness. Take my sincere advice: take up reading all of the works of St John Chrysostom; they are all available in the French language. Read the interpretation of Evangelist Matthew, of the Romans, some of it can be found in the Russian language. Until Destiny draws you out once again on the field of patriotic service, get busy (while you are still free) with a definitive education of your spirit. I offer that you study that church author,[72] who elevates the reader above all earthly things with remarkable purity and power of Christian teachings; this spiritual eagle soars above the clouds, showing the earth from that vantage point to his fledgling. It is a great achievement, I believe, for a government worker to view the earth from that height; . . . not to mention what a valuable achievement it is for a Christian person, an heir to eternity. Firmness in one's religious and moral convictions gives a person invaluable weight of character. Lack of firmness in one's beliefs and moral attitude is a great weakness, leading to instability and lack of durability in all one's actions. Fate has visited you with her blows; She said: "for whom the Lord loves He chastens" (Heb 12:16); "As many as I love, I rebuke and chasten" (Rev 3:19).

Let these blows temper you into powerful steel; become a priceless treasure for your neighbors, who surround you now and will continue to do so. Who knows the purpose of a man? It is written in the sealed books of Providence. The Cincinnati[73] left their sword for the plow and then left their plow for their sword. This is said by one who spent all his life in tribulations, who is himself covered with wounds, and is joyous over them, and thanks God for them. The banner of the Cross waves over my letter: my word always issues under this sign!— my word, either when announcing peace or issuing a proclamation of war: calls for bravery, victory, the conquest of peace, the secret army of Israel: the thoughts and feelings of a Christian.[74]

∽ Self-Delusion ∽

Holy truth comes to our heart through silence, tranquility, clarity, and peace. An inclination toward repentance encourages us toward a deeper awareness of self and toward less dependence on ourselves, fostering within us a consoling hope in God. Deceit, even when clothed in a mask of goodness, is recognized by its effects . . . embarrassment, gloom, uncertainty, changeability, amusement, dreaminess; or else [deceit] only seduces the heart—flattering it with contentment, feeling satisfied with oneself, a kind of moot, unclear sensation of pleasure. This pleasure of a self-deluded heart is like a sham tranquility, whose surface cloaks a deep and dark pool—the dwelling place of monsters. Among the already mentioned deceitful, pestilential gales, there is also cast upon the heart this terrible tranquility, this disastrous baneful pleasure, evoked by the reading of the famous book called the *Imitation of Christ* by Thomas à Kempis,[75] the Western monk who was in the grip of demonic deceit. Seductive pleasure feeds on conceit, which is born of a refined and active vanity, that blinds the mind and heart; it loves to express itself; it allows itself to depart from the correct obedience to the Holy Church, considering itself smarter than it. As with all self-delusions, it is the product of machinations of the devil and his offspring sin; this pleasure does not tolerate the sweet scent of repentance and its fruit—humility . . . both of which would bring an end to the pleasure. The Saviour of the world said: "Blessed are the poor in spirit . . ., blessed are those who hunger and thirst for righteousness" (Matt 5:3,6).

The human mind is unable to differentiate between good and evil; evil is easily masked and almost always deceives the mind. All this is

very natural: the mind of man is young and the evil conceptions wag-
ing battle with the mind have more than 7,000 years of practice . . . in
battle, in craftiness, in preying upon souls of men. The task of differen-
tiating good and evil belongs to the heart; it's the business of the heart.
But for this one needs time, the accumulation of practice with the New
Testament commandments, so the heart could acquire a refined taste
for wine that is excellent as well as wine that is counterfeit. The fact
that the heart has the task of knowing the difference between good
and evil and does not suddenly acquire this ability are both facts witnessed to by the apostle: "But solid food belongs to those who are of
full age, that is those who by reason of use have their senses exercised
to discern both good and evil" (Heb 5:14).

That is why, before one's heart acquires the skill to distinguish
good from evil, one benefits from the practiced advice of a neighbor,
a student of the Eastern Church. Only this Church is sacred and true.
Find one who sought and found in obedience to it a blessed freedom. "From obedience, said St. John the Ladder, issues true humility;
from humility is born spiritual discourse, or the mind." Outside the
steadfast obedience to the Church, there is no true humility, no true
spiritual discourse; there one finds a wide territory, a dark kingdom
of deception that creates its own self-delusion. Good can be distinguished from evil by the following features that can be recognized by
means of one's spiritual advances. In the beginning of my letter I iden-
tified these features, which are close to your spiritual state. And they
are very sufficient attributes! Little by little learn to distinguish good
from camouflaged evil. Christ is with you![76]

∼ Spiritual Battle ∼

Be courageous, fight valiantly, steadily, doggedly. Do not give victory to the enemy due to your laziness. Do not despair after your
defeat. Take up your sword again and return to the battle! The wounds
received there will heal with repentance. This is the standard for the
invisible spiritual battle.

The one to whom God wishes to grant spiritual achievement is sent into battle. Spiritual temptation batters and humbles the man, as a horse that is jabbed. The victor is permitted to enter the blessed reception. He enters, and eats, and delights at the evening meal of his Lord, as a warrior at the feast of his king, a fighter who proved his devotion to the king with his constancy, courage, with his very wounds, and his victory.[77]

∼ Childlikeness ∼

The Saviour of the world commanded those who wish to enter the Kingdom of Heaven to be like children: simple, mild, incurious, faithful, able to learn, quickly repentant in their deeds. Follow this advice of the Lord: in a short time you will feel this blessed renewal, which strengthens your soul. Renewal will take place gradually, imperceptibly. Suddenly the person will see himself changed and will glorify the All-blessed, all-powerful God. Do not complain at the brevity of my letter, do not measure it by the number of its lines. Examine your heart: if it is comforted, fulfilled, then the measure is full.[78]

∼ Struggles ∼

Why do you say that you are not worthy of my disposition toward you and my indulgence? I am nothing other than a worthless sinner, who has a critical need of God's mercy, without which my certain destiny is hell. My God tells me: "With the same measure you use, it will be measured to you" (Mark 4:24), "with what judgement you judge, you will be judged" (Matt 7:2). Needing the mercy of my God, in full measure, I have for my neighbor only mercy. Heeding my conscience, when it weighs and takes measure of my worthiness, I wish that it places me lower than all criminals. Having been judged by my conscience I cannot judge my neighbor or any one else. It is good to be at the feet of my neighbors as an image in my own mind: then the Gospel of Christ becomes accessible to man.

You are experiencing a struggle because you are in battle: the law of Christ is spiritual and it requires crucifixion. You will find consolation in the fact that humanity never entered into crucifixion without going to battle. The proof is in the God-Man. He who prayed in the garden of Gethsemane: "O my Father, if it is possible, let this cup pass from Me" (Matt 26:39). And his sweat fell on the earth, "like great drops of blood" (Luke 22:44). If you see that weakness is overtaking you, then know that the Lord is mighty and gives "power and might unto His people," as holy David says (Ps 67:36). Those people are God's own. To His people He gives strength, the ones who preserve constancy to Him in times of strife, just as their weakness leads to a collapse of loyalty in all affairs. Remember that Christ came to call sinners and not the righteous to repentance. Stand up among the ranks of the sinners, fall in humility upon Christ's footsteps, submitting to His will, charging Him with your present and future. He will pour peace and stillness into your soul and show you by this that He is near you, that His Providence stands vigil over you. One holy man said: "Blessed is the man, who knows his infirmity, because a righteous man who knows not his infirmity finds himself on a dangerous road." Another holy man said: "If Christ came not for the righteous, then I will reject my truth, as a sin, which cuts me off from Christ, and from the fact that I am a sinner, I shall find my truth, Heavenly truth, which allows me to enter before Christ and be with Him." I write you all this for your consolation, so you would see that you are indebted to Christ, that you have not come for hopelessness and sorrow but for humility and contentment. For this reason you have hope in Christ, which He will not disgrace. He is all-powerful. [79]

∽ Solitude ∽

With heartfelt pleasure I recall how you visited Sergiev Hermitage last November. There, in God's temple, during prayers and chanting of the holy services, you celebrated your saint's day, you thanked God for what had passed and prayed to Him for your future, you thanked your

Guardian Angel for his past safekeeping, asked him to protect you during your future life on earth, and till the end of this life, and till your very entry into blessed eternity—before the face of God. After the holy Liturgy you visited me in my cells; there we were comforted by our mutual love of the Lord and our discussion of Him. Consolation on earth is to see a man with the fear of God: one who brings an offering of his life and talents received from on high. To our great misfortune the larger part of humanity acts differently: God's gifts are brought as an offering to Satan.

I thank the merciful Lord, who brought me to rest in this retreat from the chatter of the capital. Already I am not unfamiliar with feelings that come upon a person living in solitude. That is why this secluded monastery handily lured me from the noisy Sergiev Hermitage. The soul is tempered by solitude, breathes into it a kind of courage, a certain manner of disdain for the world, which during contact with the world, one is unable to sense. When the soul tramples decay, rejecting corruption, then all rot, without exception, becomes perishable, and upon the scales of the heart, which is not content with anything, there settles a spiritual contemplation. This state of contemplation makes the resident of a solitary cell, it can be said, an inhabitant of paradise. It leads him into a new world, before which this world becomes very cramped, useless. In the stillness of silence the soul drifts as if in an immense space, observes what has passed, views the present, the earth, the sky, gazes on time and eternity. In such a way, in clear weather an eagle soars into measureless heights, into a transparent azure abyss.

The more extensive the space, taken up by the landscape, the more magnificent the view. Wondrous are the spaces, which man can express, describe with words, but incomparably more delightful are those which exceed verbal description, which bring joy to the heart and incapacitate the mind. They say in Switzerland there is a remarkable view among very tall cliffs; some travelers who climbed onto the terrible height were so struck by the splendor of the view, they lost their footing and fell to their death. Exactly the same effect is reached by spiritual contemplation! Whoever encounters it suddenly is cast into the abyss and virtually dies to the world! They did not revive, those cliff climbers, the overwhelmed sons of Britain: black, wooden crosses stand at the foot of the Swiss cliff. I could add that he who has died from a spiritual vision will no longer return to this world. Alas! I would say it is unfair; that is why I cannot say! Alas! Why should a man return to life in order to die! Thus Solomon came to life in order to die! So also Judas came to life to die! Many have come back to life to die! Alas! How weak we are, how changeable! . . . I look upon our weakness, gaze with tears in my eyes! . . . My eyes search for solace, for consolation—and suddenly they turn to the monastery, to solitude! There, there it is far less dangerous! . . . Strive there my soul! . . . Run! . . . If your feet are inadequate for a fast moving stream, take wing! Carry on! . . . Fly! Save yourself from the jaws of the beast: the world! Be like the blessed woman, the same who fled to the desert, the same who was seen by the seer of mysteries of the soul—John.[80] His feet are likened to the sober mind of the Lord, while his wings are his faith: he flaps them, those magnificent wings, which carried him over jungles, seas, steppes, and mountains . . . all these were given him by Christ. Him will we ask for our faith; this example was given us by the Apostles; they said and prayed: "Lord, increase our faith" (Luke 17:5).

May the Lord grant us winged faith that soars over the sea of life and enters into a blessed harbor: Heaven.[81]

∼ Solitude ∼

Myself? I need nothing! What I need is for my wretched soul. I have asked to be dismissed into solitude.

I will give you a little account concerning solitude. This is a quiet, peaceful death before our actual repose comes. It is the indispensable lot of every person; for sinners and slaves of the world it is a cruel lot. In solitude, impressions left by objects in the world are gradually smoothed over as the mind slowly loses its communication with the world. The mind gazes on the world as if from the other side of the grave, as if from the afterlife. To understand this for yourself think about China. Then look at yourself and ask what references do your mind and heart have to that country? You will see in your soul that your concepts are unclear, from hearsay, abstractions foreign to your life. They are gathered from viewing objects and interaction with them. Try as you might to have sympathy with these objects you will see that your heart is also lifeless toward this country, as if in a fictitious place or found only in tall tales. That is how the world seems to a recluse, to an inhabitant of a far-off, distant monastery. All living in the world appear to him not as permanent inhabitants but as travelers. Exactly! We live, we wander. Some go humbly on foot, others canter on horseback, or rush about in horse-drawn coaches; the end is the same for all. However, the inhabitant of a solitary place like a monastery sees little of the world with his eyes, about as much as the resident of St Petersburg thinks or is concerned for China. More absorbing, more meaningful, and more selectively is the man from the monastery focused upon the world in which he has settled: that world is eternity. The gates to eternity have opened wide before the astonished eyes of his soul, and he gazes hungrily into these immeasurable spaces, drowning in them; his mind's eyes flicker over the newly revealed, heretofore unknown till now, and completely unknown spectacle; his vision is chained to what he sees and cannot detach itself. Eternity! . . . That is where all ages past have flowed; into this gulf millions of people disappeared, taking the place of their pre-decessors on the face of the earth generation by generation; before eternity, before the views of this gulf, the world was born, humanity multiplied, tribes were formed, different peoples, kingdoms; before the views of this gulf of eternity many flourishing kingdoms turned into deserts, many great cities leveled to the ground grew into the earth and were covered by it; before the gazes of eternity unpopulated deserts, dense woods, and impenetrable swamps became flourishing habitats of society, for populous, educated noisy individuals. . . . Upon these generations and generations of people she gazed and still gazes indifferently, with cold sternness—eternity. Nothing satisfies her and nothing will sate her—eternity. Everything inside her must disappear: all her victims; upon everything she gazes like the hot spring sun shines upon the fragile, weak spring snow. . . . And upon eternity gazes, staring in his silence, in the stillness of his solitude: the hermit. Tutored by this spectacle, the hermit acknowledges, calls all things temporary, mere vanity, as he learned through Holy Scriptures. The hermit is convinced that the purpose of man is not for this earth but for heaven. That same heaven is revealed to us in the Gospels, identifying who the celestial residents should be. Each day His true servant [the hermit] wrestles hour by hour with this law of God on high, asking his mind and heart if they have shifted their attention someplace aside. Are they perhaps serving another function, a different will: one that is dark and evil and perishable. In such a life of contemplation heaven descends upon the earth, and in this vale of darkness, suffering, and tears comes consolation and blessings of the Heavenly Kingdom. [82]

∼ Repentance ∼

No one will humble a mentor as much as those who are being mentored. This is everyone's fate. It follows, you need not be surprised at what happened; do not be embarrassed by it. This means your soul benefited! And your present letter is somehow well coiffed, like the head of a small peasant after his little bath, so very humble!

Your previous letter frightened me! So smart, so full of ideas, high-minded, luxuriant!—as if a whole Guards Corps was parading on the Tsaritsyn Meadow! I did not dare answer, no matter how I read it. It horrified me; it could not be answered. Stepan needled me, coerced me, just like a farmer repeatedly urges his underfed little nag to pull the plow on his land, giving her no peace: "Why don't you answer N!" No and no. I could not respond! And nags, it seems, have their own personality.

About the following I did not want to write, but since I started to write, there is nothing to do but to answer this also. Repentance, which, as you wrote in the previous letter, you were able to touch upon, but still it was only a self-flattering dream to you. You thought about it repeatedly, yes, and listened a lot. You are smart, yet you are not repentant; inside your head you daydreamed and built there a story-book castle. And these difficulties are all my fault: I read you something that was not up to your strength and thus took you off course. "You will know them by their fruits (Matt 7:16)," said the Lord. What fruit did this condition bring you that your soul was flattered by? The fruit was pomposity, all empty in interpretation; empty pomposity led you out of your normal, ordinary condition! You wrote to the great elder. And he, as one who lives in Heaven, did not understand that you are writing about a blockhead. He answered confirming that you should live in your (imaginary) repentance, expecting the vision of repentance to be active in you as it is in him—the same vision, the same divine grace of God, as is given to monastics who already excelled in the practice of silence. Christians who live in the world must not touch advanced monastic exercises, especially the exercise of silence. And the Lord Himself commanded: "Nor do they put new wine into old wineskins" (Matt 9:17). New wine will burst old wineskins, overflowing and destroying them; spiritual exercises of monastics, when taken up by laypersons, can lead to their self-destruction and bring spiritual destruction to others.

Repentance is most appropriate for a pious person who lives amidst the world: he must account for his sins and his conscience every evening. And that is enough! If a Christian will try to live according to the commandments and will check himself every night, then little by little he will acquire a humble spirit, which is still far from achieving the kind of repentance that brings—visions. You achieved (pardon the country terminology) only folly, proud folly![83] Folly is well known to me, I am subject to folly endlessly: that is why I warn you of her.

About offering advice there is no need for you to go there, just refuse with humility. When you will be coerced, then say lightly, I leave that work to God. You are very saintly: just the man suited for a crucifixion! But you do not know how to crucify someone: you just torment them in vain. You want to gain everything by yourself and with your mind, but it is necessary to gain with faith and with God.[84]

∼ Guidance ∼

Calm down! Life on earth for a Christian is dissolved in consolations and temptations. God's Providence has made it so! Consolations support you on your road to God, and temptations make you wiser.

The company of, and discussion with, righteous men brings you substantial benefit. However, in order to be an advisor, to be a guide for someone else, it is not sufficient to be righteous; you need spiritual experience and above all else you need spiritual anointment. That is our instruction from Holy Scripture and the Holy Fathers. A pious advisor but an inexperienced one can sooner bring embarrassment, rather than benefit to those he advises. It is extremely difficult to find a spiritual advisor not just among laymen but also among monastics, someone who would weigh and measure the soul, so to speak, of the one who needs guidance, and from that domain bring appropriate advice. These days spiritual guides and advisors more often offer advice one finds inside oneself or in a book. The former is the one most beneficial and effective; that advice resides near the soul seeking sanctuary. The conscience speaks, so take one's own advice; the soul senses that. St Isaac said: "Nothing is more beneficial, than taking one's own advice." However, any unfamiliar or alien advice, even if it consists of the kindest and reasonable words, brings the soul only suffering and disturbance. The soul senses the inconsistency and strangeness of this advice. "There are"—say the Scriptures—"those who wound with a sword as they speak, but the tongues of the wise heal" (Prov 12:20 LXX).

Turn more to reading the Holy Fathers; let them guide you, remind you of the virtues, and set you on the way to God. That kind of life belongs to our times: it was predetermined, committed to us by the Holy Fathers of latter ages. I complain about the extreme lack of God-enlightened guides and counselors; they command the zealots of piety to take heed to the writings of the Holy Fathers in their life. "And the counsel of the saints is understanding" (Prov 9:10).

Try not to become scatter-brained. If you should become involved in scatter brained activity due to your debility, common to all us humans, do not fall into despair. To not be responsive is not given to men living on earth, neither for a resident of a distant monastery nor a secluded spot. Changeability and the emotions are active within each person—as well as within the strictest ascetic. Even more so for one living in the midst of the world, amidst all temptations, it is impossible not to be distracted. Do not expect of yourself the impossible; do not demand of your soul that which it cannot give. Heal your distractions with repentance, and when you fall short of your virtues restore them with a contrite spirit. May God bless you![85]

∼ Self-Knowledge ∼

Fast-flying time has rapidly approached the end of 1847, will soon fly over this boundary and the year through which we lived, will enter into the count of years gone by, never to return. From among the countless events of the year, some will be recorded on the scrolls of human history for a whole century; some will be remembered for a half century; others will keep for less time; the larger part will plunge into oblivion, sink, get buried, and disappear.

Quickly the 47th year [of the nineteenth century] raced by; just as rapidly the 48th year will speed on; soon many other years will flow past, devouring each other, superseding the one that came before. We will unnoticeably fly through the course of our life on the wings of time and invisibly arrive at the very gates of eternity! I age—it seems to me that time has become more hurried! It hurries, and hurries! . . . Stop! Allow us to look inside ourselves and discover the will of God more fully to prepare ourselves for eternity, yes . . . for eternity! One does not heed the inexorable! The mind does not consider worthy such pleadings. They are below its dignity. It flies! . . . People! God has commanded you: "See then that you walk circumspectly, not as fools but as wise, redeeming the time, because the days are evil" (Eph 5:15–16). Before stepping on the threshold of the 48th year, I bring you most sincere, heartfelt wishes and all kinds of blessings, especially those that are true spiritual benefits, which come with faith in Christ, the ones God has inspired you to seek. Acquire them with all honorable deeds! At the foundation of all deeds needs to lie the truth, just as at the underpinning of each building there must be a solid keystone! Truth is preserved in the Sacred and Holy Writings revealed by God for men. The structure of virtues that does not rest on such a foundation is completely impermanent and useless.

I am very glad that you like Moscow, especially because of the sacred places with which that ancient Christian city is so rich. But even in this splendid place one must watch over the heart illuminated by Sacred Writings and the writings of the Holy Fathers, and not by our own light, damaged by our fall, infected by delusions or by means of some other deceptive light. You write: "You cannot know, what is happening in my soul. It seems to me, that man himself, if he wishes to penetrate his own soul according to his conscience and observe its movements, he can manage that best by himself. 'As for the first statement, I agree: due to my own sinfulness and blindness of mind which comes from sin, I do not see myself and see others even less. For that reason I try to probe, penetrate the writings of Holy Scripture, accepting them in the sense that the Holy Fathers teach, as the Holy Church accepts them, and not as the Scriptures are presented by demons and their followers. And demons interpret Holy Scripture with the purpose of ruining and deluding those who listen to them. Perhaps by the light, true light, which pours forth from the Gospels and the Holy Church, I might see a little of myself, will see my own darkness, will see my own blindness!' My heart is lead astray, and lawlessness permeates me. My soul is occupied with fear" (Isa 21:4) says the prophet Isaiah as he sees himself. Seeing oneself comes from being poor in spirit [humble], and not from self-satisfaction or self-reliance.

The second half of your above-mentioned words frightened me! There is something dangerous there! I do not hesitate to write you the words of the venerable Dorotheus, which just came to me: "The enemy hates the voice of assurance: inasmuch as he wishes our ruin. See how he loves when we rely on ourselves: that is how we help the deceiver when we are self-reliant. I know no other ruin for a monk, that when he believes in his own heart. Others say: man falls either this way or that. I, on the other hand, know no other reason for a man's ruin except this very same. Have you seen the one who is ruined! See for yourself and follow him. Nothing is heavier, nothing is more ruinous," etc. If you care to see the whole article, read it for yourself in Abba Dorotheus' book, the article is titled "*O that you should not rely on your own mind.*"

May the Lord preserve you from all invisible nets of the lord of this world and save you with the glory of His Holy Name.[86]

∼ Testing ∼

Please accept my most ardent greeting on the coming holiday and the New Year. May God allow you to spend the next year and all those that remain of your life in a God-pleasing way, in contemplation of eternity, and in tasks that contribute to its attainment. Earthly shades are already leaving! Time has come to stop chasing them, as a little boy chases after golden-winged butterflies, running across a flower-strewn meadow! It is time to think, to consider thoroughly what is important, of eternity! He who is busy as one should be with eternity, he who constantly practices reading the New Testament and the writing of the Holy Fathers, who teaches us how to correctly understand the Gospels, who thus instructs us in the will of God is blessed and perfect. In accordance with these he corrects his pattern of thinking, is aware of the movements of his soul, and heals all his faults and passions with penance. A Christian who lives in the world should not read the Holy Fathers who wrote for those living in monasteries. What use is it to read about virtues which one cannot achieve in the world? There can be no benefit, perhaps even some harm may come of this exercise and may result in the person being moved to engage in spiritual reverie, which does not suit the layman at all. This state of reverie can lead to a period of self-flattering ideas that promise high spiritual achievements; and with time will bring depression and melancholy to the soul when it becomes evident that no such achievements are possible. They are always constantly distracting us from good deeds that come our way, will render our life empty and unproductive. The Christian whose lot is to spend and end his life in the world should read the Holy Fathers who actually wrote for the benefit of all. Such are the writers, whose compositions were written in the Russian language or translated into the Russian language, such as St John Chrysostom (340–407), St Dimitry of Rostov (1651–1709), St Tikhon of Voronezh (1724–1783), Nikifor of Astrakhan (?–October 28, 1682), Georgi Zatvornik (1789–1836). Here is an abundant field for reading! A plenteous spiritual pasture upon which Christ's sheep can feed till they are satisfied!

I am happy and join you in your joy, seeing from your last letter that your son's health is improving. Those whom God loves, some he accepts, some he whips and chastizes, and then He removes the punishment. One cannot draw near to God without being tested. Untested virtue, said the Holy Fathers, is no virtue! If you see someone, honored by Orthodox people as one who does good deeds, and he lives without any ordeals, a man who is successful according to the eyes of the world know this: his good deeds, his Orthodoxy, are not accepted by God. God sees in those deeds something unclean, abhorrent to Him. God looks upon the unclean deeds of man with indulgence and heals them using various methods. He turns away from the one in whom He sees demonic uncleanliness. Loving you and your son, he brought you closer to Him and allowed you to experience sorrow. You can be sure of this from the fact that as the sorrow dissipated, both you and your son understood that your "way to God became clearer and more intimate." I see this also from my own experience: I used to speak to you more superficially, lightly; now something is moving me to speak with you more deeply, to offer you spiritual food of a stronger variety, food that will give you more strength and mobility. And you, seeing God extend His mercy to you, try to accept and preserve it as is meet.[87]

~ Speech ~

"Blessed is the man whom Thou hast chosen and taken unto Thyself" (Ps 64:5).

Glory be to God, Who gave a blessed ending to your eldress! May He give all of you a blessed departure from this world of calamities and receive us in His light and joyous eternal abode, prepared for His true servants. Until that time comes we need to endure a variety of assaults for many reasons, especially from one that comes from original sin, which lives in us since the fall. In comparison with the last mentioned kind, all other assaults are of little consequence.

In your last letter you slandered me. Wonderful you, folks from St Petersburg. Now you are trying to reach the "residents of an unnamed monastery" with your slander! You write[88]: "I am very glad, that you ordered me not to speak to anyone about religion, etc." That is not true! Here is what I wrote you, word for word. "Do not engage in the giving of 'advice', but humbly refuse to participate in this activity. When you are coerced into making a comment, say something light and leave the rest to God, etc." To speak about religion and give advice are very different things: you must understand! I did not forbid you to speak of religion but said you should do so with the fear of God, with extra care and moderation. Not placing a great burden on your neighbor's shoulders is not bad. To burden your neighbor with a great weight can serve to damage him for the rest of his life, making him incapable of anything. I say this to you with heartfelt tears, from seeing through bitter experience. May God preserve me from advising you to hide what little treasure you have acquired of God, which you received not without suffering by the special mercy of God. Now there is a variety of knowledge in our life, but the knowledge of the truth has departed from people. [89]

⟿ Struggles ⟿

The Holy Church, in its God-inspired and blessed hymns calls the Holy Spirit the Comforter, calls the Son of God Comforter; and the Father who ineffably begat the Son and from whom the Holy Spirit unfathomably proceeds, Comforter. The Comforter is a Spirit; The Comforter is the Son; The Comforter is the Father. If its rays are light and fire, then the sun from which the rays flow is also light and fire.

The Holy Trinity, the Lord, glory to Thee! Glory to Thee, O Lord, who gave us life, who gave us salvation, we who sit in the shadow of death. You gave us knowledge of Truth and comfort, which flows from the resting upon us of Your Holy Spirit, Who leads us to Your Holy Truth, that is Your Word. Having known and received Your Holy Truth, we came under the influence and guidance of the Holy Spirit. We the inheritance of the Lord, His portion. At the head of the mentioned knowledge and impressions, not recognized by Truth, is Satan. In Satan's wake are his angels who will share his fate. They will feed from the earth all the days of their lives and walk on the palms of their hands. This fate descended upon them from the Judge of all, God. Their lot is to have a carnal mind, and their vestment the dilapidation of Adam.

Holy Truth, the Word of God, says: "We must through many tribulations enter the kingdom of God" (Acts 14:22). In our time, we have neither martyrdom nor great monastic struggle, but rather many daily trials. Our lot as Christians in the last days are seemingly trivial, insignificant sorrows. God has scales! Before Him, on His scales each sorrow is worthless, each sorrow is unimportant, however large it actually is to us—because His power and blessing can turn a great sorrow into a great delight. Thus even a small sorrow can have before Him all the weight of a great sorrow. All depends on his blessing: He can receive any sorrow when it is borne by man with gratitude, with humility, with thanksgiving.

The physical illness that befell you make it a means by which you give thanks to God, as a virtual offering and may the Lord accept it, just like a censor, filled with sweet-smelling incense. Your incense is your thanksgiving.[90]

∼ Death ∼

God calls you to him so you gain the knowledge of Him and through this takes you into eternal bliss! Now He calls you more clearly, more loudly, and with fresh determination. In the beginning the calling of God came to you mysteriously by way of an unfathomable attraction of your soul to the servants of the Word, to the hearing of the Word of God. And the servant of the Word spoke in words bereft of flattery, bereft of self-gratification! Now this call is marked by the sudden taking from earth of one of your family members: your son; he moved from a time-bound existence to eternity; he became the forerunner for other members of the family. Eternity took possession of all humanity; all are awaited in her boundless bosom!

I do not say "do not cry"! No! I do not say that! Give your tears freedom, spill them abundantly, enough so that your heart will be filled with them to satisfaction, so that you do not put out your faith, the gentle submission to Providence, the humble selflessness. Crying is beneficial, when it is dissolved in one's hope in God: tears comfort the soul, soften the heart, opening it to all sacred, spiritual impressions. Grief, unconnected to devotion, fails to bear blessed fruit, breeding instead malignant, mortal fruit! From this kind of grief are born despondency, despair, physical mortality as well as death of the spirit! No! you are not descending into this sorrow! You are invisibly supported by the powerful right hand of God! It led you into days of lamentation, so that during those days you would plunge deeper into yourself, wash yourself with holy ablution, your tears, so that many sighs would rise from your breast, be carried to Heaven, and clear the way so your soul could rise to Heaven. God's chastisement visited you, a disciplining dissolved in mercy, the kind of punishment sent by God to those, whom he wishes to draw closer to Him, and not those whom he scourges to bring down

His enemies. You were visited by a punishment couched in mercy! See for yourself how from the midst of darkness and sorrows sent by Him shines the light of God's mercy! Death is the unavoidable tariff for all of us mortals; each person needs to pay it sooner or later. Who in your family was given this tariff to pay?—the meekest, blameless youth! To him death is a sure resettlement into a blessed existence!—The youthful Angel is now in Heaven: there he will draw your gazes to his blessed dwelling place, and your eyes, washed with tears, will look with hope, look with joy. You will often look at the unblemished, sacred Heaven. He will call upon you the blessings and comfort of God.[91]

∼ Tribulations ∼

Never has my soul been so full of fellowship for you, as presently . . . I look with pity at you the pilgrim who endured shipwreck in the sea of life, cast out by a fierce wave onto a tidewater shore . . . On this shore . . . is a peaceful abode of monks . . . a harbor away from the storms of life . . . I come closer and see: this pilgrim, sprayed with a cold wave . . . my old acquaintance! And the first thought, the first response: to give shelter, to give warmth to this wanderer, to comfort my friend, and if my hand has the means to give help, to lay that help into his hands, to carry it to his feet! . . .

These are the feelings born in my soul upon reading your letter! . . . Do not search in the heading of my letter any worldly title, having replaced it with "the sign of Christ." May the sign of Christ wave over my words . . . And you took your place under that sign! The chief of crusaders says: "For My yoke is easy and My burden is light" (Matt 11:30)—Long has been the call for you to come under this sign!—Now you are cast down under its protective cover by force, by a furious wave. God was gazing on that wave!

Blessed is your action: you did not deviate to the left or to the right and in the hour of your tribulation you rushed into His Church, into the holy abode. And God received you . . .

Not for amusement is man put on this earth! Not for amusement . . . It is not unimportant why God created man in His own image
and likeness! It is not of no consequence that the Son of God redeemed
fallen man with His blood! We need to give value to this bounty of God!
We need to recognize the worth of the all-holy Blood of God-who-became-Man! Those who pay only superficial, fleeting attention to this
bounty, do not give full value to these things. All their soul's attention
becomes drained by their bustling about, concerned with temporary,
mortal matters. And those who spend all their lives dedicated to God
have done nothing, brought nothing worthy by comparison with the
bounty of God! One, only one is worthy to stand before God: the spirit
filled with contrition and humility. This quality of man is the only
worthy merit recognized by God Himself. Our spirit can stand in this
disposition when it renounces all amusement. I do not advise you to
depart from the external circle into which you were placed by God's
Providence. These ties of yours are sacred ties. They have a sacred seal
placed upon them by the blessings of God, evoked by the holy mystery and their accompanying prayers. In your solitude may your soul
be dead to the world; may it be your holy abode—and may it be the
dwelling of all Gospel virtues. May amusements be replaced by what
is substantial and may the shadows be replaced by truth. There is no
other path to God, except through thorns of tribulation. He who is
approved by God steps up to the treasury of all blessings, temporary
and eternal. Whomever God wants to draw closer to Himself is given
tribulations. The wave that cast you into the land of the cross was sent
to you by God, who loves and chooses you—sent like the storm and
the whale were sent to the prophet Jonah.

If the merciful Lord returns me to the seaside monastery of
St Sergius, I will hope to see you there, to recognize that you are
strengthened and comforted with the comfort and strength of the
Lord. A long time now your soul selected my soul as your haven of sincerity. Even now your soul is not left without that haven, half-wrecked
by the waves, moved by constant and fierce storms far from the safety
of the harbor . . . May the word of the incarnate God be celebrated

over us, who said: "For where two or three are gathered together in My name, I am there in the midst of them" (Matt 18:20).[92]

∽ Repentance ∽

The Holy Orthodox Church recognizes that there are no human sins that the Blood of our Lord God and Saviour could not wash clean. It does not matter how many times the sins of men are repeated: the Blood of God-made-Man can wash them clean. The sins of the whole world are meaningless before the all-holy Blood of the incarnate Lord, spilled for our sake. "But He was wounded because of our lawlessness, and became sick because of our sins. The chastisement of our peace was upon Him, and by His bruise we are healed" (Isa 53:5). Only he who rejects the healing and salvation as a gift to him and all of mankind, he shall remain unhealed. So abundantly has the mercy of God been poured upon us that the heaviest sin, repeated by man a thousand times, can be smoothed over by his repentance. Repentance— faith, repentance—the recognition of redemption and the Redeemer! Repentance—the acceptance of the service of the Redeemer by faith in Him! Repentance is selflessness! Repentance is the acknowledgment of the fall and death, which engulfs all of humankind! Repentance is the renunciation of all human virtues! Repentance places all hope on the Redeemer! Only the rewards of the Redeemer have any worth, immeasurable value! Without worth, with the least value are the virtues of mankind! They inherit their value from their faith in the Redeemer, when they are the expression of it, the rendition of His will! Repentance compensates the shortcomings of man's virtues and appropriates to him those of the Redeemer! God gave us repentance to supplement our weakness. Oh, how varied and great is our debility! Another man hates his sin but is so accustomed to sin, so powerless to fight against it that he cannot cease to fall into the hateful, squalid sin, carried away by the force of a dominating habit. This unfortunate slave of sin has one refuge—repentance! No matter how often he is confronted by a moral disaster he can enter this refuge and repair there the crushed vessel of his soul. Church history has preserved the following discussion between a certain monk who suffered from sin and one of the great saints of God, abundantly endowed with spiritual gifts, who by virtue of these gifts received the title of "Great": the monk asked venerable Sisoes the Great: "Father! what must I do? I fell." The elder replied, "stand up." The monk said to him: "I arose, and fell again." The elder replied, "stand up once more." The monk said: "How long must I stand up and fall again?" The Great elder replied "until you will be taken from this life." You will find this story in the book *Memorable Stories about the Saintly Strugglers and Blessed Fathers*; it also can be found in the *Lives of the Saints*, in the life of the venerable Sisoes the Great, for the 6th of July. One must presume that the saint gave such an answer to the man, who had an unfortunate habit for sin which was apparently insurmountable. One meets people who are subject to this affliction. The word "fell" expresses the notion that the monk's sin was heavy, deadly.

However, one needs to know that God gave us repentance entirely to help us with our weakness, not to indulge us in our sin. God's gift must not be used for evil, it must be handled reverently, discreetly, and carefully. "Whoever hopes for repentance, and repeats 'his sinful falls,'" said St Isaac the Syrian, "behaves cunningly in relation to God; such a man meets unexpected death."

One must meticulously care to keep oneself generally from all sins, large and small, which are expressions of enmity to God.

Despair is the heaviest sin. This sin despises the all-sacred Blood of our Lord Jesus Christ, denies He is all-powerful, and rejects the salvation He has given us. It shows that in this soul there ruled self-reliance and pride and that faith and humility are foreign to her. Furthermore, above all other sins, one needs to keep oneself from despair, as from a death-delivering poison or from a wild beast. I repeat—despair is the most evil sin among all sins. A fully developed despair usually expresses itself in suicide or actions identical to it. Suicide is the heaviest of sins. He who commits suicide has denied himself repentance and all hope of being saved. The Holy Church does not serve any kind of memorial over him, does not reward this death with liturgical singing, and does not permit that he be buried in a Christian cemetery.

Besides suicide, there follow other deadly sins such as murder, adultery, heresy, and others like them. These sins, although less fatal than suicide, and the despair which leads to it, are still called deadly. Those who commit these sins still have a chance for repentance and being saved. Nonetheless he who abides in these sins is held to have a soul that died; he who abides in these sins is not allowed to participate in the Holy Mysteries of Christ nor to participate in the Holy Services. If death comes to him before he has repented in these sins, then his eternal downfall is doubtless. The repentance of a man can only be truly recognized, when he leaves his sin behind. Only then can he be allowed to be in union with Christ when he participates in the Holy Mysteries! That is why one must guard against the gravest sin— despair and suicide—and guard oneself against the deadly sins, with a firm and determined will in your soul not to fall into them. If by some misfortunate sequence of events he falls into a mortal sin he must not despair. He must turn once again to God who gave us medicine for the soul, repentance, which retains all its power and validity to the very end of our lives.

There are sins considered not deadly: some are heavier, others are lighter. One needs to learn to stop the heavy sins and then the lighter ones. For instance: a non-deadly sin is gluttony; another is the love of food delicacies. Overeating is more gross and woven in with more serious consequences than the love of delicacies: that is why one first needs to break the habit of overeating and then deal with the love of sweets. In summary, the non-deadly sins also are as follows: gluttony (overeating), love of delicacies or sweets, love of luxury, empty talk (careless chatter), empty laughter, and other sins which grow in excess can approach the deadly sins in their intensity. Sin that takes possession of a person is called a passion. A passion is subject to eternal suffering, say the Fathers. That is why we must not dismiss the non-deadly sins, being especially mindful that one or another sin does not grow into a passion. For the purification of oneself from such sins and for better self-awareness, the Holy Church recommends that each Orthodox Christian participate in the mystery of holy confession no less than four times a year (in the extreme at least once a year). Holy confession brings two benefits: it brings forgiveness from God in the commission of sins, and it tends to protect us from falling into the same sins all over again. "The Soul," says St John of the Ladder, "having the habit of confessing our sins, refrains from a repeated fall by recalling our confession, being held back as by a bridle. Those sins which are not confessed, are conveniently repeated, as if committed in darkness."

There are sins, committed by word. They should never be considered of little import! The distance from a word spoken in jest to a criminal word is a small distance! "For by thy words you will be justified, and by your words you will be condemned" (Matt 12: 37), said the Saviour. The tongue committed great offenses: it spoke of the renunciation of God, blasphemies, false oaths, slander against one's neighbor. The renunciation of Christ and blasphemies are added to the gravest of mortal sins.

There are sins, committed by our thoughts, by feelings of the heart, by bodily movements. All of them are not small, all show enmity toward God! But when the mind and heart delight in the sin, love to imagine it with elaborate color, and excess, such a secret sin of the soul is close to the real thing committed by one's deeds.

A person needs to avoid any sin whatsoever, with all his strength. Those sins committed out of weakness through deed, word, or thoughts and all one's emotions need to be brought to God daily through repentance. It is best to do this by following a prayer rule, before going to bed. Every year he must purify his conscience at least four times a year with the mystery of holy confession. If he falls into committing a mortal sin, he needs to immediately confess this before his spiritual father. May the Lord preserve you from the great emotional distress of mortal sin and give you the strength to distance yourself from similar sins, large and small. Amen.[93]

⌒ Falsehood ⌒

Here is a spectacle that deserves bitter tears: Christians who do not know what Christianity is about! This spectacle is encountered constantly by our eyes; rarely are our eyes comforted by the opposite, consoling vision! Rarely do our eyes meet among the countless throngs of those who call themselves Christians, people who are Christian by name as well as deed.

The question, suggested by you, now follows: "Why," you write, "cannot they be saved . . . the pagans, Muslims, and so-called heretics? Among them are the kindest of people. To lose these kindest of people would be most displeasing to the merciful God! Yes! This is distasteful even for the soundest reasons of man! And heretics are the same Christians. To consider yourself saved, and members of these other faiths unsaved, that is insane, and extremely arrogant!"

I will try to answer you in as few words as possible, so that wordiness does not cloud the clarity of the point. Christians! You speak about being saved, and you do not know what being saved means or why humanity needs it. Finally, you do not know that Christ is the only means of our salvation! Here is the true teaching about this subject, the sacred teaching, of the Ecumenical Church: being saved means a return to communion with God. This communion was lost by all humankind by virtue of the fall of our forefathers. All humankind is ranked among all creatures that are lost. Being lost in perdition is the lot of all humanity, both those who are virtuous and those who are villains. Conceived in lawlessness, born into sin. "But he refused to be comforted . . . 'I shall go down into the grave to my son in mourning'" (Gen 37:35) said the patriarch Jacob about himself and about his saintly son Joseph who was chaste and beautiful! In the Old Testament, not only sinners but also the righteous came down to hell at the end of their wanderings on earth. Such was the power of the good deeds of men. Such was the worth of good deeds in light of our fallen nature. In order to restore our communion with God, in other words, for us to be saved, it was necessary there be redemption of our sins.

The redemption of humankind was completed not by an Angel, not by an Archangel, not by some sort of higher, but limited and created beings. It was completed by the limitless God Himself. Death, the lot of humankind, was paid for by His execution; the inadequacy of human merits was replaced by His infinite worth. All good deeds of man were too inadequate and replaced by one powerful good deed: our faith in our Lord Jesus Christ. The Lord was asked by the Jews: "'What shall we do, that we might work the works of God?' Jesus answered and said to them, 'This is the work of God, that you believe in Him whom He sent'" (John 6:28–29). We need but one good deed to be saved: faith. Faith is the deed. Through faith, only through faith we can enter into communion with God by means of the Mysteries He gave us. In vain and mistakenly you are thinking and speaking, that good people among the pagans and Muslims will be saved, that is they will enter into communion with God! In vain are you viewing the contrary thought as if it were something new, as if it crept in as an error! No! That is the constant teaching of the true Church, as well as the Old and New Testaments. The Church always affirmed that there is only one means of being saved: a Redeemer! The Church recognized that those who practice the greatest virtues of our fallen state still go to hell. If righteous persons of the true Church, the saints who shone with the Holy Spirit, prophets, and miracle-workers, who believed in the coming Messiah, foretold the coming of the Redeemer, descended into hell, then how do you wish for pagans and Muslims who appear to you as good people, they who have not acknowledged and not believed in the Redeemer, how do you expect them to be saved? Being saved can only be achieved, I repeat, by one means: faith in the Redeemer! Christians! Know Christ! You must understand, you who do not know Him, that you rejected Him, believing you would be saved without Him, through some sort of good deeds! He who expects to be saved without faith in Christ rejects Christ, and perhaps not knowing this, you fall into the mortal sin of blaspheming God.

"Therefore we conclude that a man is justified by faith apart from the deeds of the law" (Rom 3:28). "Even the righteousness of God, through faith in Jesus Christ, to all and on all who believe. For there is no difference; for all have sinned and fall short of the glory of God, being justified freely by His grace through the redemption that is in Christ Jesus" (Rom 3:22–24). You object: the Apostle James certainly demands good deeds, he teaches "that faith without works is dead" (Jas 2:20). Examine once more what the Apostle James demands. You will see that he demands, as all God-inspired writers of Holy Scriptures, deeds of faith, and not good deeds of our fallen nature! He demands a living faith, confirmed by the deeds of a new man, and not the good deeds of fallen man, which are repulsive to faith. He brings up the example of the Patriarch Abraham, a deed, which revealed the faith of a righteous man: that of bringing his only son as a sacrifice to God. This was not a good deed at all according to human nature: it is a good deed, as the fulfillment of a commandment of God, as a deed of faith. Look deeply into the New Testament and generally into all of the Holy Scriptures: you will find that they demand the commandments of God be followed, that this action is called doing deeds, which fulfill God's commandments and result in a living faith, an active faith: without this kind of deed your faith is dead, deprived of any movement. Contrary to this you will find that good deeds from a fallen nature, which originate in emotions, in your blood, from impulses and tender feelings of the heart are forbidden, even rejected! These same good little deeds appeal to you among the pagans and Muslims! For them, even though they rejected Christ, you wish to give them salvation! Strange is your judgment from a sound mind! From what, by what right do you find and recognize this sense in yourself? If you are a Christian, then you must have a Christian understanding of this subject, and not a different self-willed or clutched knowledge from somewhere! The Gospels teach us that by our fall we acquired an unreliable reasoning power that the mind of our fallen state, no matter what merits it has by nature, no matter how much it is distinguished by higher learning in the world, still retains the qualities attributed to it by our fall and remains unreliable. One must reject this mind and submit to the guidance of our faith: under this guidance in its own time, and with struggles in piety, God gives the loyal servant of His a true reason, a spiritual reason. It is this reason that can be called commonsense reason: it is distinguished by faith, so excellently described by the Apostle Paul in the eleventh chapter in his epistle to the Hebrews. The foundation for spiritual reasoning is God. On a hard rock this reasoning ability is created, that is why it is not shakable, does not collapse. What you call common sense we, Christians, recognize as ill-conceived reasoning, pitiful and lost. It cannot be healed, and all knowledge issuing from this reasoning can only be rejected and cut off with the sword of faith. If we are to recognize your reasoning capacity by some means, on some unknown, shaky, uncertain, constantly changing basis, then this reason, just like your common sense, will certainly reject Christ also. This is proven by experience. What does your common sense say to you? That to acknowledge the death of good people, who do not believe in Christ, is repulsive to your common sense? Moreover, such a death of virtuous people is repulsive to the mercy of such an all-beneficent Being as God. Of course, you received a revelation from above about what was repulsive or not repulsive to the mercy of God? No! But your common sense tells you this.—Ah! Your common sense reason! Where, with your rationality, did you get the idea that with your own limited human mind you can grasp what is repulsive and not repulsive to the merciful God? Allow me to express your thoughts: the Gospels, otherwise known as Christ's teaching, otherwise called the Holy Scriptures, and again the Ecumenical Church, have revealed all to us that man may know about the mercy of God. This revelation exceeds all human sophistication, all achievements of men that are otherwise unavailable to them. Vain are the mental vacillations of man, when he seeks to define the infinite God! When he seeks to explain the inexplicable, to subordinate God to his own reasoning. Such a goal is a satanic undertaking! You call yourself a Christian, and yet do not know the teachings of Christ! If you have not learned from this blessed, divine teaching the unfathomable nature of God then go to school and listen to what children are learning! They are taught by mathematics teachers about the theory of infinity, which states that an infinite sum is not subject to those laws which govern finite sums—numbers—that the results of infinite sums may be completely opposite to finite numbers. And you wish to determine the laws that govern the mercy of God, saying: this is agreeable to Him—and this is repulsive to Him! It may be in accord or not with your common sense, with your understanding and emotions! Does it follow that God is obliged to understand and feel, as you understand and feel? Because that is what you demand of God! This is total lack of judgment and a completely arrogant undertaking! Do not blame the judgment of the Church for your shortcomings of common sense and humility: that is your deficiency! She, the Holy Church, only follows steadily the teaching of God and about God's actions, revealed to us by God Himself! Obediently the true apostles of the Holy Church follow her, being illumined by their faith. We believe that we are allowed to know about God only what God has given us to be revealed about Him! If there were another road to the Knowledge of God, a road, which we could lay down with our own efforts, then we would not have been given revelation. Revelation is given to us, because it is necessary for us. Vainglorious and duplicitous are our own mental exercises and wanderings of the human mind.

You say: "Heretics are the same as Christians." Where did you get such an idea? In reality can anyone call himself a Christian and know nothing about Christ? Can he by his most extreme ignorance decide to call himself the Christian as the same as a heretic and not distinguish the holy faith of Christianity from the fumes of God-blaspheming heresy! True Christians reason about this differently! Countless hosts of saints wove their martyr's wreath, preferred the fiercest and prolonged suffering, dungeon, exile, rather than to agree to participate in a heresy that blasphemes their God with false teaching. The Apostolic Church always considered heresy to be a mortal sin, always recognized that man, infected by the terrible disease of heresy, to have a dead soul, a stranger to blessings and salvation, to be in communion with the devil and his fall. Heresy is a sin of the mind. Furthermore, heresy is a sin of the devil, rather than of man; heresy is the daughter of the devil, his invention, an impurity not unlike idolatry. The Holy Fathers usually call idolatry as lawlessness and heresy as godlessness. In idolatry the devil assumes a godlike pride to himself from his blinded human participants who are committing their main sin, blasphemy of God. Whoever reads the "Acts of the Church Councils" attentively, he will surely see that the character of heretics is fully satanic. He will see their terrible hypocrisy, immeasurable pride. He will see their behavior, composed of endless lying, that they are committed to countless low passions, and when they have a chance, determine to commit all manner of horrible crimes and malfeasance. Especially notable is their irreconcilable hatred for children of the true Church and a thirst for their blood! Heresy is closely spun with an exasperated heart, with a terrible defilement and damage of the mind. It is stubbornly lodged in an infected soul and it is hard for such a person to be healed from this affliction! Every heresy contains a blasphemy of the Holy Spirit: it either blasphemes the dogma of the Holy Spirit or the actions of the Holy Spirit, in either case it directs its blasphemy at the Holy Spirit. The essence of every heresy is blasphemy against God. Saint Flavian, Patriarch of Constantinople, marked with blood his witness to the true faith. He spoke of the decision of the Council of Constantinople about the heretic Eftichios in the following words: "Eftichios, until now a priest, an archimandrite, is completely guilty, by virtue of his former actions and his explanations of the misconceptions of Valentin and Appolinarius, guilty of a stubborn following of these misconceptions and their blasphemy of God, and furthermore, that he even failed to listen to our counsel and instructions to accept a proper course of teaching. That is why, we grieve and sigh over his ultimate death, we announce from the face of our Lord Jesus Christ, that he fell into blasphemy of God, that he is deprived of any priestly anointment, deprived of communion with us and the management of his monastery, giving notice to all, that henceforth anyone found in discussion with him or visiting with him, will himself be subject to excommunication." This definition is recognized by the general opinion of the Ecumenical Church about heretics; this definition is recognized by the whole Church, confirmed by the Ecumenical Church of Chalcedon. Eftichios' heresy consisted in this, he did not confess that Christ has two natures of God, as the Church confesses, he ascribed only one nature of God.

You will say only! One person's response to St Alexander (Patriarch of Alexandria, a person who is clothed in a powerful office of this world) about the Arian heresy was amusing and grievously pitiful for its consequences. This person advises the patriarch to preserve the peace, not to stir up any disputes, which are so onerous to Christianity, just because of a few words; he writes that he finds nothing condemnable in the teachings of Arius, perhaps some difference in the turn of a word only! These turns of words, remarks the historian Fleri, which "have nothing condemnable," reject the divinity of our Lord Jesus Christ! Subvert, in other words, all Christian faith! Wonderful: all ancient heresies, under a variety of changeable deceptions, sought only one goal: they rejected the Divinity of the Word and sought to falsify the dogma of the incarnation. The latest heresies seek more ardently to reject the actions of the Holy Spirit: with terrible blasphemies they rejected the Holy Liturgy, all the mysteries, all, all, where the Apostolic Church always recognized the action of the Holy Spirit. They called these: human creations, and more grossly: superstitions and delusions! Of course, in a heresy you see neither banditry nor theft! Perhaps that is why you do not consider heresy a sin? Rejected here is the Son of God and rejected and blasphemed is the Holy Spirit! He who accepts and carries the blasphemous teaching about God, who does not declare the blasphemy an act of banditry, does not steal, who even performs good deeds with his fallen nature. He is a wonderful man! How can God refuse him salvation! The whole reason for your latest quandary, just as for all the preceding ones, is a deep ignorance of Christianity! Do not think that this ignorance is a shortcoming of little importance! No! The consequence of this ignorance can be fatal, especially now when there are countless little books with Christian titles but with satanic teachings. Being ignorant of true Christian teaching you can easily fall for false teaching, then accept it with blasphemous thinking, adopt it for your own, and thus earn for yourself eternal death. A blasphemer of God will not find salvation! The misguided thinking, which you expressed in your letter, is already a fearfully slanderous witness for your salvation. Such thinking is equivalent to a rejection of Christ! Do not toy with your salvation, do not bandy with it! Otherwise you will cry for an eternity. Get busy with reading the New Testament and the Holy Fathers of the Orthodox Church, not Teresa, nor the Franciscans, nor similar Western crackpots, whom their heretical Church presents as saints!; learn from the Holy Fathers of the Orthodox Church how to properly understand Holy Scriptures, how to conduct your life, what feelings and thoughts are proper for a Christian. Learn about Christ and Christianity from Holy Scriptures and a living faith. Before your fearful hour comes, in which you will stand before God, learn proper righteousness offered freely by God to men through Christianity.[94]

∼ Death ∼

What unexpected news came to me with today's mail! Konstantin Fedorovich, in the prime of life and mature manhood, promising so much for his native land, for his parents and all his family, essential to all who knew him, suddenly left the field of earthly life! His dust is already covered with earth and resting in the Sergiev Hermitage! Long will he rest there! He will be awakened and come to life at the sound of the trumpet announcing the Resurrection of all men! As for his soul may it find peace in blessed, quiet, and light-filled mansions of Heaven! May his soul's path be strewn with her own piety and the piety of his parents! Thence may her path be strewn with the prayers of the Holy Church, those of his father and of his mother, of his widowed spouse, and those of the weak and uncomprehending orphans, the infants, his children!

A heavy sorrow has befallen you, an uncommon one, but one commensurate with the fortitude of your soul! You will need to clothe yourself in the armor of living faith that breathes into your heart firmness, courage, humility, and obedience before God's decision. You will need to communicate the strength of your soul to your body weakened through its physical structure, though not weak in its devotion to God,

Daria Mikhailovna: you are his mother! You will need to take the place of your son's role in the family: to step into, once more, the duties of a father, occupied with educating children. An unexpected and heavy cross fell upon your shoulders! Though it was sent by God, it came without warning, approached, and suddenly, with all its weight settled on your shoulders. Blessed are those shoulders, which are able to feel the Cross of the Lord upon them! Blessed is the soul that will accept and carry the Cross of our Lord with generosity of spirit.

The Cross is a sign of being the chosen of God; it is the hallmark of Christ. With this hallmark Christ marks His Own! The beloved angels of God are represented with this sign on icons of Christ Almighty! "If you see someone," said venerable Mark the Struggler, "someone who spends his life in constant wellbeing, know this: a merciless judgment awaits him upon his death. He is forgotten by God." All saints confirmed this infallible truth that he who spends his life without struggles is forgotten by God. Do not seek, said one of them, Christian perfection in virtues among men: it is not found here on earth; it is mysteriously preserved in the Cross of Christ! No matter what good deeds were done by the Saints, they considered them incomplete and inadequate, if they were not crowned by the Cross of Christ, which was not marked by the sign of Christ. Only those will complete this pathway, cleared by the Cherubim, who will hold scrolls, certified by the hallmark of Christ.

The mercy of God visited you during your life in the form of a happy family and in the blessings of your service to the Tsar and native land. The very same mercy of God is found in the cross you were sent to bear. God's punishment is not the same as human punishment! The wrath of God is not the wrath of men! God punishes and loves! He calls you to a closer knowledge of Him. Brief knowledge of the great of this world brings short-lived honors and imaginary riches; similar knowledge of God gives us eternal benefits, the ability to see God's glory, and participate in it.

I always looked at you with the eyes of my heart, with a deep heartfelt emotion, which is hard to achieve, whose existence is not even suspected by those who live their life carelessly. I believe: God gave me this ability so that I may offer you a small reward in your time of need for your abundant love. I gaze at you from this distant monastery: I see the very same thing! Distance does not prevent me from seeing with my heart. I constantly sensed in you, in your soul, some moral task, which was not fully resolved. It needed to be resolved! God's Will can now be seen more clearly: it pleases Him that your soul should bring forth spiritual fruit for your eternal granary, appropriate to your means and strength, planted in this soul. That is why he brought you this challenge. It pleases Him that you should be closer to Him, to know Him better.

Konstantin Fedorovich is almost the same age as I, a little younger than I. Since we met, a full quarter century has flown by; at the time he was in the uniform of a page and I in a uniform of a cadet. The first thought that flashed through my mind after reading of his death flew right into my heart, "he also went into the monastery." Now you, as an unbiased judge [can see]: Does it matter whether to go into a monastery a few years earlier or a few years later? A monk is the same man departed with a living word! His word is from another world! From the same world, where the soul of the departed went. I am a living corpse, who acquired a new cohabitant in the Sergiev Hermitage—your son, the dead man, who sealed his lips forever. May God give me the ability to speak for him and for me a "word" from that other world, a word of comfort, a word of salvation!

Tears flow profusely, the pen does not stay in my quivering hand. May Christ be with you! He will strengthen you and with you all your family.[95]

∼ Doubts ∼

You doubt the existence of hell and eternal agonies? "This is not consistent with such a merciful and good being, as God."

Ah, my friend! How can such a weak, limited creature, like man, judge all by himself about God, an infinite being, more elevated than

any [human] achievements and judgments, to come to positive conclusions about God by looking inside yourself? Leave all your personal
reasoning and believe with all your heart what we are taught in the New
Testament. The Saviour Himself said: "And these will go away into ever-
lasting punishment, but the righteous into eternal life" (Matt 25:46) and
in another place it says: "in Hades, he lifted up his eyes" (Luke 16:23).
The Saviour said that there is hell and there is eternal agony; what are
you objecting to? If you acknowledge this objection, that means you are
doubting in the true words of the Saviour, and you reject them. Should
you reject even one dogma of Christ, then you reject Christ. Think well
about this: your doubt is not a lightweight sin. If you take it to yourself,
you will realize your doubt with words and you will fall into a mortal sin. One word of faith can save and one word of doubt can destroy
your soul. One of the robbers already on the cross, in the hour of his
death, confessed Christ and opened the doors of paradise for himself;
the Pharisees, who rejected the Truth, blasphemed the Holy Spirit and
were lost. "For by your words you will be justified, and by your words
you will be condemned" (Matt 12:37), announced the Saviour. If you
will permit your reason to object to the teachings of Christ, it will find
a thousand thousands: your reason is inexhaustible if we permit it to be
infected by a dislike for Christ. Little by little your reason will reject all
dogmas of Christianity! This is not news! This is the product of unbri-
dled, self-willed judgment; reason has bred countless atheists in the
world, blasphemers! By their outward appearance, to the inexperienced
eye, they appeared to have brilliant minds, appeared unshackled and
free, revealed the truth and had shown it to other people. But consequences showed that their truth is imaginary, a most awful, pernicious
delusion. Their false ideas are washed in rivers of blood, and the rivers
did not purify them! It is frightening to spot a thought with falsehood:
human blood does not have the power to wash away these fierce stains.
For such a purification of these unclean spots, men required the blood
of God-who-became-man. Mankind received this blood, washed itself
in it, and was purified! Guided by the hand of faith, mankind came out
into the light again of the true Knowledge of God and of itself. Mankind

arose from a deep, dark chasm of the physical and falsely named reason. This reason calls men again into the chasm—admonishing them to join the journey into the self-destructive abyss again! What is so surprising? Man has preserved his nature in paradise, filled with sweet aromas and delights created by God, man did not stop entrusting his attention to the flattering words of the devil. My friend! You are a Christian, a member of the Eastern Orthodox Church; keep true to the spiritual body, of which you are a member. Keep communication with the Holy Church, to which you belong, preserve your spiritual virtue, as the priceless treasure that it is. Because of your weakness do not delve into judging the dogmas: that is a deep abyss, a dangerous sea; in that sea many have drowned, even strong and self-reliant swimmers. Only those can swim unscathed along the wondrous waves of theology, whose mind has been nurtured by the right hand of the Holy Spirit. According to the advice of the Apostle Paul, expel all imagination that diminishes the mind of Christ. Do not enter into argument, nor into reasoning with doubts and objections posed by a rebellious mind; sever the heads of these snakes with the sword of faith, as soon as they show their heads from their pits! This is a straightforward matter, a sure matter! This matter is worthy of the man, who once and for all joined forces with Christ. Before union [with Christ] there was a place for reasoning; after union with Christ, such argumentation is equal to criminal conduct. Nothing, but nothing should violate or shake your fidelity to Christ! Oh, it is more tolerable for one who never entered into union with Christ than for one who betrayed Him. Bow your neck to the good yoke with humility; conduct your life with piety; attend church more often; read the New Testament and the writings of the Holy Fathers; perform charitable acts for your neighbors: in good time Christ's Holy teachings, which breathe with sanctity and truth, will be absorbed into your soul. Then no doubts will approach your soul. Christ's teaching is wondrous Divine teaching: it will become accessible to the human mind by means of faith alone. To explain the supernatural by human reasoning is an insane undertaking that is apparently unable to depart from the general, ordinary, natural circle of experience. The products of this insane undertaking are inconsistency, countless objections, rejection of the supernatural, even when it is Divine. By their actions people often contradict themselves! They protect their eyes from specs or sores, but their mind, that is the eye of their soul, they do not think to protect. Thus they litter their mind with all kinds of rubbish. The Lord commanded us to preserve the mind, because it is the leader of the man. If the mind goes astray from the true path, a person's entire life will become a delusion. It does not take much for the mind to go astray: all it takes is some kind of false idea: "The lamp of the body is the eye. Therefore when your eye is good," says the Lord, "your whole body also is full of light. But when your eye is bad, your body also is full of darkness. Therefore take heed that the light which is in you is not darkness" (Luke 11:34). We completely fail to follow this holy legacy; we do not watch that our light, that is the mind, does not become dark and throw into it all kinds of litter; our mind becomes decidedly cloudy and pours darkness on all our behavior, on all our life. One can ask why does your soul give birth to imaginings that war against God, imaginings that are full of harmful faithlessness and philosophizing? I am certain you have read your fill of all kinds of empty foreign books, listened to all kinds of insubstantial judgments about religion, which are so plentiful in our times, when we are so lacking in true knowledge of religion. "Nothing is so effective in directing man to blaspheme God, as the reading of heretical books," said Isaac the Syrian. Drop this disorganized reading, which fills your mind with disorienting, perverse concepts that deprive your mind of firmness, independence, and a clear vision, and turn you into a state of skeptical shivering. Get busy with the substantial study of the Holy Fathers. Do you belong to this Church? It is your obligation to know it as it should be known.[96]

∼ Purity ∼

When traveling down the road, which runs along a wide plain, we encounter a branch-filled tree. It casts a most luxurious shade and with what joy travelers stream toward this tree; sweet is the rest and friendly conversation for them beneath the cool, wide, and broad shade of this tree. Such a shelter, such consolation, is offered to those who travel the road of life by the holy Cross of Christ. The thrice-blessed tree, upon which the fruits of our life were born, is the incarnate God, the Life, and Giver of life. Under this canopy of the Cross, it is pleasant to converse with you.

Listen to the following sacred story: "A certain man came to the great saint Pimen complaining that he sees in his own good deeds a measure of sinfulness. The elder told him the following parable: Two landowners once lived close to each other. One of them planted a little wheat, even though the seeds were not pure; and the other, giving in to laziness, did not plant anything. At harvest time, the first man collected enough harvest, even though it was not pure, while the other collected nothing. Which of these landowners will have enough to eat? The man answered: the one, who planted seeds, even though not pure ones. The elder replied: let us also plant a little, even though it is not clean, so that we not die of hunger."

God granted you the capacity to look into your heart and there you saw a mixture of mental imaginings and spiritual truth. The story I quoted you can already comfort you to some extent: you can see why it was given you. To comfort you some more, listen to the following: God alone can grant a sacred purity of heart to those who believe in Him and come to Him with repentance. He does not demand from us, just beginning our road to Him, this exalted purity, free from any stains. Prior to achieving purity comes our vision and consciousness of our impurity. And that is already a gift from God, about which we pray to receive on our bended knee: "Lord, allow me to see my sins!" But he, who sees his own impurity, must cry over it and ask the all-powerful and all-blessed Physician to heal us.

The Holy Spirit is the true guide of Christians. His channels of communication were the prophets, apostles, and other saints of God: He spoke through them. May he be your director and "He will guide you into all truth" (John 16:13). Step into this blessed guidance, then you will draw upon the benefits for your life only from the Sacred Writings penned by the Holy Fathers of the Eastern Church, the one truth.[97]

∿ Repentance ∿

"Long did my soul wander" (Ps 119:6). The merciful Lord gives His servants all in His good time, and to me also, a wanderer, the shelter of repentance. May He give me this precious gift! And I will share these treasures, earned through repentance, with my friends who love the Lord. The gift of repentance is a pledge for eternal blessedness. Purified with repentance may I enter paradise. Entry will not be allowed to those whose garments are not whitened with repentance. I shall see there those who like myself love the Lord, and I will fall with them before the feet of Christ, who did not hide from us the village where repentance dwells, in which are found the precious pearls of salvation. The merchant who wishes to buy this village must sell all his possessions in order to purchase the village of repentance. May I be that merchant! May I be the owner of this spiritual gift in order to obtain my salvation and those near to me! My soul sighs, yearning for a deep, uninterrupted silence, outside of which one cannot find an abundant, full repentance. I give myself to the will of God! May He do His will in me and all the rest of us.[98]

∿ Fear of God ∿

My heart, orphaned on this earth, heard an echo in your soul, seeking to know God, as He is, and to bow before Him, as God. Since He humbled himself for us, having taken the form of a lowly servant for reasons of inexpressible love for us, then we have no right to forget this before Him. We need to approach Him as servants before God, just like creatures before their Creator, "with fear and trepidation to One who gave us salvation," according to the testament of the apostle. His indescribable majesty naturally induces an awesome fear among all who approach Him, as well as those who are closest to Him. The prophet David said: God "is fearful to those who are near Him," to the glorious Seraphim, and the fiery Cherubim, who unable to look at the glory that exceeds the light of the creatures shield their fiery faces with their wings, and ceaselessly sing: Holy, Holy, Holy Lord of Sabbaoth!

How will a gloomy sinner stand before the grand face of his God? Only if he covers himself from head to toe with garments of repentance. Without these garments, devastated from head to toe with putrid lesions of sin, it is more natural and righteous for him to be in the dark, in the fires of hell, rather than before most holy God. Hell! Now that is an appropriate place for sinners.

Let us dignify ourselves with Hell, so that God honors us with Heaven.[99]

∼ Sorrows ∼

Weariness comes over me for two reasons: after I become involved in some task, word or sinful imaginings, and when I have not been practicing repentance, even though I was engaged in useful activity. Then my soul feels something lacking, feels a deprivation: and from the feeling of being deprived I feel sorrow.

This sorrow is healed with repentance and prayer, "a contrite and humble heart God shall not despise" (Ps 50:19). "I remembered God, and I was glad" (Ps 76:4).

Look inside yourself. In the above-mentioned reasons for sorrow, will you not find a reason for your own sorrow? Use the healing practice: prayer, dissolved in repentance.[100]

∼ One Thing Needful ∼

The prophet David, king of an extensive kingdom and owner of great wealth, cried unto the Lord: "I am a pilgrim upon earth, O hide not Thy commandments from me" (Ps 118:19). Certainly this is the "one thing" that is needed, as the Lord said, "and Mary has chosen that good part, which will not be taken away from her" (Luke 10:42). But all other earthly benefits will be taken from you both at your death and after death.[101]

∽ Seeing Clearly ∽

I am offering you a sacred, extremely ancient story: "Three monks, sincerely devoted to good works undertook for themselves the following pious exercises: the first set out to make peace among those who were bickering. He was inspired to do this by the words from the Gospel: 'Blessed are the peacemakers' (Matt 5:9). The second decided to devote his entire life to serving the sick. He was drawn to this work by the Lord's words '[when] I was sick and you visited Me' (Matt 25:36). The third went into silence and the desert. He who set out to make peace among the bickering had a very meager success. After becoming fatigued, he came to his brother who was devoted to serving the sick; but his brother was also weakened with fatigue and unable to continue his service. Then the both of them agreed to visit their friend in the desert. Coming to the third monk, the first two explained their sorrow and begged him to tell them what he had gained through the vow of silence? The desert dweller, after hesitating silently a bit, took some water and poured it into a vessel, saying: look into the water. They looked and saw nothing, because the water was cloudy. After some time passed the host again asked them: now that the water has remained still a while, look at it again. When they looked at the water, they saw their own faces, as if in a mirror. He said to his friends: 'he who lives among people cannot see his own sins, being distracted by the entertainments of the world; when he comes to practice silence, especially in the desert, then he begins to notice the sin that lives inside him.'" One needs to see his own sin, then wash it in repentance, and acquire a pure heart, without which a person cannot perform any good deed completely, with a pure conscience. Seeing our own sins is not that easy, as it may seem on the outside, according to the first superficial look. In order to acquire such a vision, one needs much preliminary information. One needs a detailed knowledge of the law of God, without which one cannot know anything positively, such as what specific acts, words, thought, feelings belong to the truth and which are sinful. Sin often takes on the appearance of truth! One needs to know in detail the properties of a man, in order to know what are the sinful sores of the mind, what are the sores of the heart, what are those of the body. One needs to know what does the fall of man mean? One needs to know what properties are found in the heirs of the New Adam, in order to see what and why are our shortcomings. One requires much preliminary and important information, in order to receive a detailed and clear vision of one's own sins! That kind of vision is received following true silence. The soul arrives at such a vision that is akin to a clear mirror-finish surface of water; in such a surface, a man sees not only his own condition but, according to his spiritual achievements, the condition of his neighbors.

My solitude is interrupted by frequent internal and external rumors; my water, on the whole, is clouded! Very rarely, rarely does it assume a certain mirror-like surface and still only for an instant! In that brief moment there appears a most attractive vision before the eyes of my mind. I see an endless mercy to me from God, I see a chain of unbiased blessings from Him. For what reason were they poured upon me? I am perplexed. How did I pay my Benefactor for these blessings? With endless sins. I look at my sins and am horrified as if I were looking into a frightfully deep abyss, from one look into it my head begins to spin. What if I begin to measure this abyss? I begin to measure it with sorrows, with sighs, and with cries! I am still crying. Suddenly the sorrow in my heart is replaced by amazing joy: as if someone says to my heart: "God, the Unfathomable Benefactor, is unsatisfied with His blessings; He also wishes to bring you into Heaven, to make you a partaker of eternal delights." I believe that every blessing, no matter how great, we can expect from the measureless goodness of God. I believe that all my being is immersed in delightful joy.[102]

∼ Silence ∼

I spend my time in idleness, due to the method of healing that
I use. It brings me appreciable benefit but uses up all my time.
Unpleasant preoccupation with the body, which, in spite of all the
care it gets, must surely return to its state of dust, into its own soil,
from which it was borrowed by the Creator. I look into myself: realize that due to illnesses and circumstances I was made for solitude;
cold and dead is my heart toward external services. With one blow
I would like to be able to cease my association with society! And I
would do that not for myself, not for people, but so that my intentions and enterprises would be pure before God, who said: "No one,
having put his hand to the plow, and looking back, is fit for the kingdom of God" (Luke 9:62).

However, the judgment of God and human judgment are very different: so said a certain honorable father, especially gifted in his ability to reason spiritually. I do not know what God has assigned to me;
and I, having examined myself, find that I am not fit for social duties,
and more capable in areas of solitude, to which I have grown accustomed, having spent many years almost hopelessly tied to my cell.
In seclusion one can easily indulge in travel to the spiritual world, to
which my mind and heart have already moved. I have no strength to
return them to earth! And their move from earth occurred without
my knowledge. I did not imagine them moving and did not know that
this was possible and suddenly saw them already transported. Then
my heart and mind already gazed upon the earth as upon strangers in
a foreign land. Having visited the wonderful land of the indestructible
[of things eternal], a world of blissful peace and light, my heart and
mind turned away from the land of shadow, from dissension, disputes,
ceaseless turmoil, from the land where good is mixed with evil! A dark
country is the earth! Earth is a land of exile for criminals, who dese-
crated paradise with their sin, who are guilty of disobedience to God,
defiant in their relationship to God, having traded this relationship
for one with the devil. On the earth, all is hostile toward man, and

he himself is in constant strife with himself. Earth is a vale of exile, a valley of original suffering, with which begin our eternal sufferings, the deserved punishment for offending the One who is endlessly gracious. The earth is our exile, that is why the Redeemer came here; He redeemed our measureless sin with a limitless price—His blood. The earth is our exile: that is why the Redeemer raises those who accepted His redemption from the earth to Heaven. Heaven is the true home of man: the road to Heaven needs to be accomplished within ourselves. We need to see who holds power in this world!

We borrowed the poison of sin from them, in all its petty aspects and diverse forms. Having sectioned off all that is foreign to our nature, we will be left with ourselves, with our own pure nature. This cleansing is accomplished in us by the "Word of God," which reveals to us the properties of the New Adam and the ulcers of the old Adam. The all-blessed Holy Spirit, having seen our clean state, will come down upon us, shall cover us with His chrism and light, will change us, mark and initiate us into the blessed tribe of the chosen, into the generation of the second man, who shall be the "Lord from heaven."

Having been marked by the Holy Spirit, we will no longer fear the powerful, dark, and malicious of this world. We will walk through their dark and thick regiments into the light of truth and find in its bosom the foretaste of future bliss. Whoever completes this journey on earth through the inner man, whoever frees himself from the captivity of sin and is betrothed of the Holy Spirit, his soul shall experience the separation from the body without obstacles and the ordeals of airborne tormentors. All of this, and much else, is inexplicable using the language of the earth, and man learns through [exercises in] silence. The Holy Spirit nestles in the one who practices silence correctly, accompanies him, announces the secrets of the Kingdom of God, in order to nourish the silent one abundantly with knowledge and spiritual sensation so that he may feed his brothers who are hungry and thirsty for this knowledge.

The teachings of the Spirit is living knowledge: light shines from Him, life breathes in Him. The teachings of people form the fallen nature of man. It is dark, dead, and has a false light, it flatters [our] hearing and emotions of the heart, preserves in the listeners, multiplies the darkness in them, intensifies the dominion of death. A wondrous miracle occurs during the teaching of the Spirit: when the Spirit is the teacher. He who enunciates the word of God and he who listens to it both share in the knowledge of life. All glory belongs to the mysterious Teacher; he who enunciates the word of God senses that he enunciates not his own word but the word of God. He who listens senses that he is listening to the word of God; all his attention is drawn to the spiritual power that enlivens him; while to the human word which is clothed in the word of God, his heart remains cold. In the temple of his spirit, the idol called "I" is toppled and cast forth; in that temple, purified from the filth of desolation, flows the sweet scent of the Holy Spirit and can be heard relaying messages of the Holy Spirit.

What do you think—what kind of sensation will embrace the man who speaks the syllables of the Holy Spirit, feels within himself the action of the Spirit? That sensation is natural for one who stands before his Creator. Then man actually realizes that he is nothing.

Not from books, and not from men, nor from natural ingenious talents does man become a student, capable of hearing and being an agent of the Spirit! Only through the mediation of faith in Christ, through the life of Christ in himself, through the transfer of Christ's properties in himself, which properties Christ revealed to men in the sacred enunciations of the Gospel. Where Christ is, there is his Spirit, there is His Mind, His unfathomable Father.[103]

～ Repentance ～

What lightness, what well-being, what a blessed purity in one's soul when a man does not allow the formation of friendly feelings toward himself by his neighbors, but acts only as a conduit for them to holy, unblemished Heaven! When he tells God about his loved ones: "Lord! They are your own, your creatures! What is Yours belongs to You, and I am what? I am a short-term wanderer on the Earth, who arrived suddenly and just as suddenly will disappear from here." Whosoever cleanses his love of self-esteem and bias, he acquires a purified love, the love of God. In order to acquire this love it is ordained that we practice selfless devotion; that is the meaning of our Lord's words: "For whoever desires to save his life will lose it, but whoever loses his life for My sake will find it" (Matt 16:25). In these words Christ's command is coupled with a promise.

On the contrary, whosoever will decide to find his life among the seductive activities of this world, that is, he will want to act out his unclean wishes, he shall lose his life. In selfless devotion there is salvation.

Submit your mind to Christ. When our mind submits to Christ, then we need not justify either our mind or our heart. When all manner of justifications will disappear from your heart, then your mind will come into a state of contrition and tenderness: "a contrite and humble heart God shall not despise" (Ps 5:19 LXX), but expressions of justification lead to a terrible sinful death.

That is how holy David prayed and how he teaches us to pray: "Incline not my heart unto evil words, to imagine excuses for sins with men who work wickedness" (Ps 140:4 LXX). "To imagine excuses" is to justify oneself in sinful behavior. The thoughts and words, through which these sins are excused, are called "words of cunning." Cunningly the sinner tries to fool himself and others! Cunningly he tries to present himself as a just man before himself and others! To justify yourself before people, to hide one's sin before them, is sometimes necessary by circumstances, to protect a loved one, who might be tempted by our sin. To justify yourself before yourself, to deceive, to drown out your own conscience, is always lawless, always disastrous; having assimilated "words of cunning" makes a person a bitter Pharisee who is capable of any crime. Justifications for sinful behavior do not require fictitious or long-winded words; the justification that is always acceptable to God is repentance.

Every sin runs from the face of repentance; no sin can remain standing before almighty repentance. Repentance is the virtue of the

Gospel, a priceless gift of God, purchased for us with the blood of the Son of God, with the price that redeems our every sin.

Decide from the very start, if only in your mind, to abdicate from sin for the sake of Christ, free your mind from ruinous, senseless willfulness, and submit to the commandments of Christ, submit to the Gospels. The beginning of selflessness starts in the mind: having submitted yourself to Christ, He will gradually bring you to blessed contrition of heart and body.

Selflessness is frightening at the first, superficial glance; however, no sooner does a man decide upon it than he senses a remarkable lightness and freedom: lightness and freedom are witnesses to the Truth.[104]

∼ Eternity ∼

My thought is constantly crying for God, so that He allows me a path to Himself, a path of repentance. The gates of eternity have opened widely before me. I glance there into this infinite distance, into this limitless space, into these immeasurable measures. Time is reduced before me. It flies incomparably faster, in order to fall like a stream into the sea, into eternity. I peek into eternity: things temporal are not engaging. They are petty, vain, negligible. I love solitude: within it I can look into eternity more closely and spy what is needed there and prepare it in advance, before the soul leaves the body.

I am preoccupied by the Gospel. My gaze is amazed by the features of the image of God and shades of the likeness of God, as they are presented in the Gospels! "Learn from Me" (Matt 11:29), says God to men. In order for them to adopt this wondrous likeness, God became man. What indescribable beauty in the New Adam, in the Lord our Jesus Christ! What ugliness there is in me, what disorder! How many spots on me! That is how I see myself when I look in the mirror of the Gospels. I also need to get busy with the face of my soul and its various garments; before I step into eternity, I need to see that my soul has nothing in common with the enemies of God, with dark demons; I need for the Son of God to recognize in me His own likeness, just as all blessed residents of heaven are like Him. Man's likeness to God is recognized by God and will deliver to man a blessed eternity; the loss of this likeness brings with it a banishment from the face of God into the gloom of hell, into its fiery gulf, into eternal suffering.[105]

∿ Christ's World ∿

Christ's world "surpasses all understanding" (Phil 4:7), unites into one man, cleft by sin—Christ's world fulfills all our being with humanly unreachable power and heavenly sweetness, begins to descend into our soul, when it is cleansed of the passions by keeping the commandments of Christ, and by doing good deeds. In order to preserve Christ's world in us, in order to taste it fully, in order to be transformed from a former to a new man, one needs solitude. A creature left at a crossroads will eventually be plundered and stolen.

Mighty is the world, flowing from the action of the Holy Spirit. Who can withstand His appeal? From His face all passions flee; from His actions the mind and heart are transported into Heaven. Man is reconciled to all with God. He begins, so to speak, to float in the boundless space of the spiritual world and learns that the commandment of God "is exceedingly broad" (Ps 118:96 LXX). Christ's world created martyrs and venerable ones: He leads the Christian out from the power of the flesh and blood, removes the poison of sin from the soul and body, destroys the forcible influence of demons on the soul and body, introduces the attributes of Christ into the Christian, such as meekness or goodness. The soul, having sensed these properties, begins to taste a wonderful peace, a pledge and beginning of an eternal peace of the righteous in the habitations of eternal bliss.[106]

～ Divine Fire ～

Our God is fire ["God shall plainly come, even our God, and He shall not keep silence; there shall burn before Him a consuming fire" (Ps 49:3) LXX.] we are taught by Holy Scripture, but the action of this fire gradually quenches the flames of sin, fires of the soul and body. Divine fire is pure, delicate, and light. It informs the mind of the truth, and the heart of a wonderful calm, a marvelous coolness to all things earthly, with ample meekness, humility, and goodness.

Make no mistake! Human passion is not reckoned together with the actions of God's fire. Many erred and fell into a destructive delusion. Countless delusions arose from a condition of passionate excitement and seeded the earth with false teachings. Beyond these dark clouds hides the sun of truth from the world. "You will know them by their fruits" (Matt 7:16), said the Saviour about false teaching and its teachers. Where there is emotional excitement, there is no truth, nothing good can arise from that, nothing useful: there blood boils, there rises smoke and castles in the air from false reasoning. Meekness and humility, whose actions are accompanied by a refined coolness, then appear in countless blessed harvests. They are witnesses of a genuine, and true, and Divine goodness.[107]

～ Illumination ～

The teaching of the Eastern Fathers of the Church is true: it is the instruction of the Holy Spirit. I beg you, hold onto this teaching! It will guide you to a blessed eternity.

A brilliant lantern is lit by the Holy Church of Christ. It is the illumination of the Holy Spirit: do not direct your gaze to other lanterns that shed their light on other pathways. One holy pathway of truth leads to salvation. There are many who suffer, many who are followers. The one who will be saved "competes according to the rules" (2 Tim 2:5). The truly lawful endeavor is with Jesus Christ and the Holy Spirit, within the confines of the holy Eastern Church.[108]

～ Asceticism ～

Presently I am reading books in Slavonic, Russian, and other languages, consisting of "The Collection of sayings of holy desert dwellers of Egypt." These sayings are priceless pearls! A diver descends into the depths of the sea in order to fetch an expensive pearl: and the Holy Fathers disappeared into secluded deserts where they went deep into themselves, finding much that was priceless, spiritual pearls: Christ-emulating humility, youthful simplicity, and lack of malevolence, angelic freedom from the passions, spiritual wisdom, and reasoning ability: in one word they found the Gospel.

Today I read that sayings of the Great Sisoes, which I have always particularly liked and found close to my heart. One monk once said to him: "I find myself in ceaseless memory of God." Venerable Sisoes said to him: "That is not a great thing; what will be great is when you will count yourself among the least of all creation."

It is a lofty task to practice constant memory of God! But that elevated practice is very dangerous, when the ladder to it is not founded on a firm footing of humility.

See how Holy Scripture is in agreement with the Fathers! Scripture states: "Thou delightest not in burnt offerings. The sacrifice unto God is a contrite spirit; a contrite and humble heart God shall not despise" (Ps 50:18–19). Sacrifices and the same burnt offerings of people must be based upon a sense of a poverty of spirit, on a feeling of personal humility. Without this the offerings are rejected by God.

I also like a saying from the Great Pimen: "If we will always and in all things place the blame on ourselves then we will find peace everywhere." Another Father said: "We have left the easy burden, consisting of laying blame upon ourselves and took upon ourselves the heavy burden of blaming others." Such quotations are worthy of entire volumes! No one, it seems, has delved into the Gospels as much as the holy desert fathers have delved into them. They tried to put the Gospels into practice in their own lives, through their own minds and feelings. Their most distinguishing feature was their deepest humility;

the fall of man was their constant subject of reasoning; their ceaseless occupation was to cry over their own sins.

Ascetics of the Western Church took a different direction. From the time of their split from the Eastern Church her writers on asceticism fell into the most disastrous gloom of heresy. St Benedict [of Nursia] and the holy pope Gregory the Dialogist[109] are still in agreement with the ascetic mentors of the East; however, Bernard[110] distinguishes himself with a specific type of thought; later fathers have drifted even further from the Eastern Church. They immediately carried their readers away into heights that are inaccessible to novice ascetics, sweeping themselves and others away. A highly heated, often excitable dreaminess replaces in them everything spiritual, about which they have no idea. This dreaminess is considered a blessing by them. "You will know them by their fruits" (Matt 7:16), said the Saviour. Everyone knows with what crimes, with what streams of blood, with what behavior, decidedly anti-Christian, Western fanatics have expressed their disfigured form of thought, their ugly feelings of the heart.

The Holy Fathers of the Eastern Church do not bring the reader into a loving embrace or into some elevated visions. They bring the reader to an examination of his own sinfulness, his own fall, into a confession before their Redeemer, into a self-admitted cry before the mercy of his Maker. Firstly, they teach us to restrain the unclean instincts of our body, to make it light and capable of spiritual exercise. Then the Fathers address the mind, correct the train of thought, its reason, and purify it of the understanding, adopted by us since our fall, replacing it with the renewed nature of man, vividly depicted for us in the Gospels. Together with the renewal of the mind the Holy Fathers are concerned with that of the heart, about changing its habits and feelings. It is harder to renew or cleanse the heart than the mind; the mind, convinced of the fairness of new thinking, easily sheds the old and adapts to new ways of thinking. But to replace one skill with another, or one character quality with another character quality, one feeling with another feeling, one that is opposite to the first kind, is intense, relentless labor, which is an incredible struggle. The fierceness of this battle the Fathers refer to when they write "give blood and receive the spirit." That means one must mortify all sinful urges of one's body and blood and all activity of the mind and heart dependent upon on them. One must bring the body, mind, and heart under the management of the spirit. The blood and nervous system are coaxed into action by different passions: wrath, greed, gluttony, and vainglory. The last two overheat the blood among ascetics, who engage in ascetic practice without authority and in consequence lose control of their emotions and become extreme fanatics. Vainglory yearns first of all for a spiritual state, for which the person is not ready due to his unclean condition and to replace the failure at truth invents for himself a wishful state. And gluttony joins its actions to vainglory and creates in the heart a misguided self-flattery, false consolation, delight, and pacification. This condition is the condition of a pleasure seeker. All who engage in unsupervised, unauthorized ascetic exercise find themselves in this condition. This condition becomes more or less intense depending on how much they increase their efforts. Thanks to this condition, Western writers authored many books. Many readers fall upon these books with a hunger, and these authors are considered saints and spiritual persons, worthy of standing next to Holy Scripture by a blind and proud world, considering themselves enlightened to a high degree, and as a result not needing to stand by the heritage of the Eastern Church.

The Holy Fathers of the Eastern Church do not show an excitable overheated condition of the blood. They never display enthusiasm, which gives birth to excitable blood, which often in the West seeks the spilling of blood. Their compositions have the breath of genuine selflessness, that of the sweet fragrance of the Holy Spirit, which mortifies the passions. The sons of this world run away from this fragrance, just as wasps fly abroad from smoking incense. "The world would love its own" (John 15:19), said the Lord. Western writer's compositions, having been written under a condition of self-flattery, find themselves many readers, are translated more than once into the Russian language, are printed, and reprinted; they receive much verbal, written, and printed vociferous praise: that which is accomplished with deadly poison is approved and attested. Writings of the Holy Fathers are forgotten! The fact that they have been received from ancient times by the Holy Church, that they were accepted as the only correct guide to a spiritual life, is no longer given respect. Western writers criticize them, find inconsistencies, contradictions in Holy Scripture. All this has a reason: that the Holy Fathers were instructed by the Holy Spirit that they rejected the Wisdom of the world in order to acquire the wisdom of the Holy Spirit. Futile are the attempts, which, contrary to the teachings of the Apostles, inimical to the teachings of the Church, encroach upon the wisdom of the Spirit using that of this world. "He catches the wise in their own craftiness"(1 Cor 3:19). They stumbled and fell with a terrible fall. They wished to explain the "spiritual" using dark human reasoning, and this "spiritual" in the writings of the Holy Fathers seemed strange to them, seeming to contradict Holy Scripture. "Comparing spiritual things with spiritual," said the holy Apostle Paul. "But the natural man does not receive the things of the Spirit of God, for they are foolishness to him; nor can he know them, because they are spiritually discerned" (1 Cor 2:14).[111]

⟡ Wisdom ⟡

You ask me my opinion on human sciences? After the fall, people began to cultivate the earth, developed a need for clothing and many other things, which accompany our earthy wanderings; in other words, they began to have material aspirations, which distinguish our age. The sciences are a product of our fall; creatures of our damaged fallen reason the acquisition and preservation of impressions and knowledge accumulated by men during the life of a fallen mind. Scholarship is the light of ancient man, the lamp to whom "is reserved the blackness of darkness forever" (Jude 1:13). The Redeemer returned to men that "Lamp," which was gifted them during their creation by their Maker, the very one they lost after their fall. That Lamp is the Holy Spirit. He is the Spirit of Truth, who guides into all truth, experiences all the depths of God, reveals and explains all mysteries. It grants also material knowledge, when it is needed for a spiritual purpose of man. To the scientist who wishes to learn spiritual wisdom, the apostle bequeaths this: "If anyone among you seems to be wise in this age, let him become a fool that he may become wise" (1 Cor 3:18). Exactly! Scholarship is not properly wisdom but only an opinion of wisdom. The cognitive knowledge of Truth, which was revealed to man by the Lord, is gained access only through faith, which is not approachable by the fallen reason of humanity. It is replaced in scholarship by guesswork, by assumptions. The wisdom of this world, in which an honorable place is given to many pagans and atheists, is directly opposite, from its very beginnings, to the wisdom of God. One cannot be a follower of one and the other belief system at the same time; one position certainly needs to be rejected. Fallen man "is a lie," that is, an image of thoughts, a collection of false concepts and knowledge, having only the outward appearance of reason, but in their essence these concepts are vacillations, delirium, madness of the brain, struck by the deadly wound of sin and a fallen state. This affliction of the mind presents itself with special fullness in the philosophical sciences.[112]

⁓ Reading ⁓

Try to read books of the Holy Fathers, which reflect your way of life, so that you could not only admire and delight in this but apply them in your life and work. The Christian, living in the world, needs to read compositions of the great theologians, who wrote for the people, teaching them about Christian good works, commensurate with the life they lead in the material world. Other reading is appropriate for monastics living in communities; they need to read the Holy Fathers, who wrote instructions especially for this kind of life. Besides this there is still other reading recommended for practitioners of silence and solitude! The study of spiritual virtue when it is not in accord to one's way of living leads to daydreaming and brings one to a false spiritual condition.

The practice of virtuous living, when it does not correspond to one's manner of life, makes life non-productive. Life is depleted needlessly, virtue is lost as well: the soul cannot hold onto virtues for long, needing to release them because they are too costly for it. This exercise strains the strength and abilities of practitioners of lofty virtues and often damages the soul beyond repair. It can be wounded for a long time, sometimes for one's whole life, rendering the soul incapable of undertaking spiritual struggles of piety. The Lord commanded us to pour "new wine" (Luke 5:38), that is, advanced spiritual exercises and accomplishments, into "new wine skins." This means we should offer new spiritual struggles only to those who have matured in their work of piety, who have been made new and enlightened by grace. He forbad that new wine should be poured into old wineskins, forbad us to repair an old garment with a new patch. Do not think that advanced spiritual exercise will benefit one whose soul has not matured. It will not help you! No! It will distress you further: you shall need to drop the exercise, and despair will settle upon your soul, hopelessness, gloom, and callousness. In such a state of mind, you will allow yourself many sins, a large downfall from the law of God, perhaps falling into sins you have known before. "An ancient garment is not mended by new patches, because the original hole will become larger still" (Matt 9:16; Mark 2:22; Luke 5:38).

And for all monastics in general as well as for Christians living in the world it is most profitable to read the New Testament, especially the Gospels. However, one needs to read it with humility not allowing oneself personal interpretations but relying on the guidance of the Church.[113]

∽ Pathways ∽

Abide in the shelter of the truth. The enemy of the salvation of man tries to draw our thoughts from the shelter of truth by means of various phantoms of it. He knows how strong this net is. Seemingly insignificant to the inexperienced eye, the mind is attracted to the net through curiosity, with a pompous saintly name, by which our destruction is usually obscured. That is how the gullible nightingale, a little, especially curious bird is lured with food, scattered under a cage, and is caught forever into a boring life lacking freedom. False thinking is destructive: it penetrates the soul with gloom and self-delusion, making the soul the captive of the prince of this world. "And the truth shall make you free" (John 8:32), said the Saviour; evidently falsehood deprives you of freedom, subjects you to the region of the prince of this world. I wish that you be free, that the vision of your soul be clean and light, that your mind be imbued with the light of truth and pour forth a graceful light upon all your life, on all your works. "The lamp of the body is the eye. If therefore your eye is good"—said the Lord—"your whole body will be full of light" (Matt 6:22). We need to guard our mind! The mind needs to abide ceaselessly in truth. I wish this upon you sincerely from my heart! I wish this for you from an ailing heart! It is ailing because in our times very few people cleave to the Truth, having inclined their mind and heart to the yoke and burden that is easy. Very few have subjected themselves simply and obediently to Christ and His Holy Church. "Be saved," says the holy Apostle Peter, "from this perverse generation" (Acts 2:40). Steer away from the wide road, along which most people are traveling! Choose for yourself a more narrow road and a sorrowful one, leading to the Kingdom of Heaven! Learn to love the narrower path along which Wise Providence laid out your earthly path of wanderings! Make your sorrows and narrow path on this earth pleasant and sweet. How should one do this? Submit yourself to the will of God, praising the Providence of God, recognizing this will and Providence in all things that come to you, thanking God for your struggles and joys. It is time to live a truly Christian life, harnessed by all your emotions, wishes, and thoughts on the cross of the commandments and teachings of Christ. Quickly, rapidly will your earthly life shoot by you! Every man already has an eternal reward waiting for him during this brief journey on earth, for his good deeds, for his beliefs, for his sensations.[114]

◯ Love ◯

The venerable father Dorotheus, speaking of love for your neighbor, likens the Christian ascetic to lines leading from the perimeter of a circle to its center. For a clearer example, visualize a sketch! The closer the lines approach the center, the closer they become to each other. In a similar way Christian ascetics, the closer they become with God, the nearer they become to each other with true love.

Every journey of the mind and heart, when its goal is God, is infinite. "The fear of the Lord is clean, enduring forever" (Ps 18:10 LXX). The benefits from the wisdom of the Lord are infinite. The prosperity that comes from the love of one's neighbor, when its aim is God, is infinite. One lifetime is not sufficient for perfecting this spiritual journey! One cannot be fully sated with love of one's neighbor when the object is God! On the other hand, one can complete the journey, be quickly satisfied, and even be sated with love of one's neighbor when the object is only man. The fire of love demands much fuel in order to be constant and grow. When the fire is fueled by God, it is constantly strengthened, knowing no bounds; but when the fire is fed by man with his limited means, the fuel for it becomes scant, the fire dims, and is quenched. Love must be nourished by the infinite God; the food given by the limited properties of man is insufficient, even though they may be fine.[115]

◯ Self-Denial ◯

The heart can only delight in blessed peace, when it lives among the commandments of the New Testament, in a manner that is selfless. When another kind of truth rises in the heart it loses its peace.

The New Testament is magnificent and all holy! In it we see the new, god-like man; and what properties must the new man possess is revealed in Christ's commandments. Christ revealed to us His properties in the New Testament, His manner of thinking and acting. By glancing into the New Testament, looking in that mirror at ourselves, we can bit by bit recognize our shortcomings, little by little cast away our age-old beliefs and ancient qualities, replacing them with thought patterns and characteristics of the New Testament, of Christ. That is the challenge, the lesson, which each Christian should resolve, fulfill, and accomplish during his life on earth. One must imprint a portrait of Christ on our soul, lend it a likeness from its original prototype. Portraits lacking a likeness to Christ will be rejected on that universal judgment at which each person will be tested to what degree he preserved or renewed in himself the image and likeness of his Creator and God. Images, whose features are so distorted, whose attributes and colors have so lost their likeness, will hear: "I do not know you" (Matt 25:12). They will not be recognized! The Lord will reject them!

Let us begin a spiritual painting! Let us draw our attention to the image of our Lord, the head drawn back, covered with mud, scratches, and dust, inscribed over us, entrusted to us by God! The painter is Christ; His brush is the Holy Spirit. Let us prepare our soul for this painting, so that the soul, as a clean canvas, should be able to receive all the finest of features, the most tender colors and shades.

Such an image needs to be cleansed with repentance, washed with tears. In order to arouse in oneself the urge to repent, to produce salvific sadness and tears, one must unfailingly practice abstinence from all passions and read the New Testament frequently, to compare our life with the holiest commandments, to compel oneself to live up to these commandments, contrary to the wishes and impulses of our sinful willpower. A certain holy father said: "Through the practice of Christ's commandments a person learns of his debilities." Exactly: then it is revealed to us just how weak we are, how we are damaged by the fall, as soon as we begin to compel ourselves to practice the New Testament commandments. Tears come naturally after seeing our weaknesses, our fallen state. Our cries are a heartfelt emotion of repentance! Our cry, "a contrite and humble heart" (Ps 50:19 LXX), is so pleasing to God. When the Lord sees the soul being cleansed with repentance, then He begins little by little, by virtue of her purity, to renew her, with the aid of the Holy Spirit, restoring the features of His own image, the shades and colors of His likeness. Before all, He renders her with humility and gentleness "learn from Me," said He, "for I am gentle and lowly in heart, and you will find rest for your souls" (Matt 11:29). Only then can we discover holy peace, when the mind and heart plunge into the humility of Christ, and His meekness, having learned it from the New Testament. These two virtues restore order in the features of our image of ourselves, distressed by embarrassment, which cohabits relentlessly inside each person, beset by passions. The indication of order is a sacred calm. Then over the corrected features one may apply holy pigments, which bring consolation to the spiritual appearance: goodness; mercy; purity of mind, heart, and body; a living faith; no care for all that is vain. These holy pigments teach man to follow Christ wholeheartedly, with patience. Such patience is considered above all temporary sorrows, a love of grievings, such as sharing in the sufferings of Christ, love of God and one's neighbor, seeking to fulfill all duties of man toward his Creator and to creatures, like himself, urged to become one with his Creator. Deny yourself, and follow the New Testament![116]

～ Sufferings ～

Man is like the grass. It doesn't take much to mow him down.

It just takes one minute to decisively smash his health and cast his body into the grave or place him on the suffering bed of a long illness. The New Testament teaches us that no sorrow may fall upon us without the will of God. It teaches us to thank God for everything, including sorrows that come at His call. Bring your thanks to God from your sickbed, as Job used to bring his from the heap of pus covered with stinking scar tissue. Thanksgiving dulls the fierceness of your illness! Thanksgiving brings the ailing person spiritual consolation! The tutored heart, sweetened by thanksgiving, is renewed through the power of a living faith. Illumined by the sudden light of faith, the mind begins to contemplate the divine Providence of God, ceaselessly holding vigil over its creation. Such contemplation brings spiritual joy; the soul begins to give thanks abundantly, to glorify God. It begins to laud His Holy Providence, to submit to His holy will. The sickbed is often the place where one gains the knowledge of God and the knowledge of self. The suffering of the body often brings spiritual joys, and the sickbed is often watered with tears of repentance and tears of joy in God. During illness one first needs to compel oneself to thank God, then the soul tastes sweetness and peace, received by way of thanksgiving. The soul hurries there as to a safe harbor. The soul rushes there from the difficult murmuring waves of cowardice and sorrow.

"We must through many tribulations enter the kingdom of God" (Acts 14:22). Whomever God loves, to him he sends sorrows, and that mortifies the heart of the chosen one to the world, teaches him to soar near God. All struggles, including illness, bring healing to the soul and consolation: devotion to the will of God, thanksgiving to God, reproach of oneself and acknowledgment of the worthiness of God's punishment, the remembrance that all the saints completed their earthly journey in ceaseless and dire suffering. Suffering is the chalice of Christ. He who has not taken communion from this chalice is not able to inherit eternal blessings. [117]

⁓ The Knowledge of Christ ⁓

Strange thoughts come when one is in seclusion! "The ear of a hesychast hears divine things," said one holy monastic. In my worthless solitude I encounter thoughts that make a strong impact on my mind by virtue of their living truth. Not long ago I was meditating on the brevity of human life. Suddenly life appeared to me so brief that even the rest of my days on earth appeared already to be in the past. I will live some more and what new things do I expect to find on this

earth? Nothing: the same virtues and the same passions, which heretofore appeared before me in various guises and actions, will continue
to appear henceforth; the very same virtue will quietly wade among
people, unnoticed, rejected among them; the very same vice sheltered
by countless disguises will deceive people and be a dominant force
among people. Two years of life and one hundred years of life are
equally short, insignificant before eternity. Usually people see their
future life to be long-lived; only their past life seems short to them,
like a dream of the night gone by. Solitude, combined with a penetrat-
ing look at oneself, allows a glimpse of our future life as brief as well.
Brief is both the past and the future! So, what is life on earth about?
The road to eternity, which needs to be used well but without looking from side to side. This journey must be made with the mind and
heart, not by counting days and years. The mind, benefitting from
teachings about truth, can preserve a peaceful heart, humility, blessedness, patience. In short, the mind can gain the qualities of the New
man. That is why there are desert-dwellers, hesychasts, and monasteries! There are also discussions profitable for the soul and spiritual
counsel! For this purpose one also has readings of the Holy Fathers!
Prayer is also for this purpose! All Christians should live like this,
unfortunately very few do. If you cannot fully live like this, then at
least live partially like this. Your shortcomings can be healed with
self-condemnation and repentance. If you see shortcomings in yourself, do not despair; to the contrary, fight them with humility. Isaac
the recluse had this to say, remarkably: "The glory of the saints is
likened to the shining stars, amongst which one shines very brightly,
another more dimly, and another is barely visible; but all these stars
are in the same sky."

How many generations have changed places on this earth! It seems
like they were never even here. For how long were heard many powerful names? Now they are forgotten. How long has our generation
entered the platform of public life? Now a new generation is stepping
upon this platform, edging us out of the large arena onto the periph-
ery into a modest corner with other aged and obsolete. Generations of

men on earth are virtual leaves on a tree! First one set, soon replaced by another! They are ruined by the heat of the day and the winter frost, and time itself scatters them in the wind to be stepped on by other travelers.

I gaze from my solitary corner onto the noisy and restless world, tell myself and my friends: only one occupation can be recognized as truly worthwhile during our short-lived stay on earth, while our turn comes, knowing Christ, Who is both the giver of blessed life eternal and the road to that life. Christ lives in the New Testament. It is that vineyard in which Mary can find Christ. It is that faithful soul that lives in humility on the outskirts of town, outside the love of the world. There is the coffin of Christ! There His loved ones cry. They cry for Him and for themselves.[118]

～ Thoughts ～

I often chat with you about Eternity. I'd like you to understand how important it is to be aware of your pattern of thought, about your reasoning. Men are certainly led by their own thought patterns: this is our world. One must take heed to keep watch over it, so that it does not become dark, a world of lies, showing things not where they belong, not as they should appear, substituting one thing for another. "Take heed that the light which is in you is not darkness" (Luke 11: 35). It is necessary that our thought patterns be seeped in the Truth. Apart from Christ, I neither understand, nor do I know any other Truth. Were they not blind, whoever they were, at that time, before whom Christ stood in his terrible magnificent humility, and asked: What is Truth?

Hearken deeply to my words! I ask and beg you! I beg you for your very own salvation. Usually people consider that thought is somehow of little consequence, because they have little discernment as they receive their thoughts. However, from the reception of incorrect thoughts is born all evil. A thought is similar to a ship's wheel: from this seemingly negligible piece of wood, which drags the entire vessel, depends the entire direction and most certainly the fate of the entire huge machinery of the ship. "The perception in your soul seems to be good, then good counsel will guard you, and holy thinking will keep you" (Prov 2:11), say the Scriptures; it teaches us: "The beginning of Thy words is truth, and all the judgments of Thy righteousness endure for evermore" (Ps 118:160 LXX). What is this "beginning" of our words if not our thoughts. Truth is witnessed on the earth by the Holy Spirit. So said the Apostles to the Jews. The witness of Christ's Truth is the Holy Spirit. Where there is not witness by the Spirit, there is no confirmation of the Truth. He who wishes to sinlessly follow the Truth must abide with the teaching, which appears and is witnessed by the Holy Spirit. Such is the teaching of the Holy Scriptures and the Holy Fathers of the Eastern Church, the only holy, the only Orthodox, and true. All other teaching is alien to the Truth of Christ, the Truth, come down from Heaven by virtue of the extraordinary mercy of God revealed to men, "sitting in the dark and deathly shelter," sunken in gloom and deep depression of self-delusion, ignorance, fallen, and in perdition.[119]

～ Truth ～

The apostle correctly said: "For with the heart one believes unto righteousness, and with the mouth confession is made unto salvation" (Rom 10:10). One needs to confess the truth with the mouth, and when possible, with deeds. The truth when it is confirmed by words and deeds, so to speak, is realized, becomes the property of the man. That is why, once it becomes significant this way it becomes collateral for salvation.

You were convinced that the only sinless road to salvation is the unwavering following of the teachings of the Holy Fathers, together with a decided rejection of any other teaching, an avoidance of one's own reasoning, until one's mind is converted from being carnal and internal to being spiritual. Having recognized this truth with your mind and heart, confess it with your mouth. Give God your oath that you will be guided by the teachings of the Holy Fathers, avoiding all teaching that is not witnessed by the Holy Spirit and is not adopted by the holy Eastern Church. Having confessed the truth of God with your mouth, substantiate it with good deeds; having given an oath, fulfill it.

Have no fear of this oath! It must be given by every Orthodox son of the Church; it must be demanded of every son of the Orthodox church at the sacrament of confession. Among questions, which are required to be asked of someone for confession, the first place goes to: "Tell me, child: do you believe, that the Church is catholic, apostolic, originates from and issues from the East, and spreads over the whole world from the East, and inhabits the East constantly and without interruption 2) And have you no doubts about this tradition? 3) Tell me, child, have you been a heretic or apostate? 4) Did you keep company with them, visit their temples, listen to their teachings, or read their books?"[120] The reading of heretical books and paying attention to their teachings are heavy sins against your faith, a sin of the mind, ailing from pride. That is why it throws off the yoke of obedience to the Church, in the search for a sinful, mindless freedom. And today such a sin is no longer considered a sin! Now you are permitted to indiscriminately read heretical writers. The Church has thundered anathema against them! But blinded sinners do not heed the thunder of the Church, or they heed it, only to laugh at the warning of danger from the Church, in order to judge the Church as superstitious or barbaric. Audacious and incredible insolence! It is expressed in print.

True Christians of all times meticulously protected themselves from the deathly poison of heresies and similar false teachings. They held tenaciously to the dogmatic and moral teachings of the traditional Church. They not only had Orthodox faith in the Holy Trinity, but they conducted their life, spiritual struggles, and their morality according to the traditions of the Church. A distinguishing feature of all the Holy Fathers was their unswerving allegiance to the moral teachings of the Church, and they taught that only that was a true guide, which followed all teachings of the Eastern Fathers of the

Church that only their writings are a witness to. Those who think to lead their fellow men according to their own worldly reasoning, from reason that has fallen, no matter how brilliant, then he himself is in a state of self-delusion and brings his followers into the same state of self-delusion. The Holy Fathers established unchangeable conditions for those who wish to be saved: to follow the moral teachings of the Church. These individuals were instructed to live pious and God-pleasing lives under a true spiritual leader or be guided by the writings of the Holy Fathers in accordance with the life of each individual. With the passing of eight centuries from the birth of Christ, the Church Fathers begin to complain at the shortage of spiritual leaders and the appearance of false teachers. In the absence of worthy spiritual guides, they instruct us to turn to the writings of the Holy Fathers, to steer clear of books written outside the bosom of the Church. The further time moved away from the appearance of Godly light on this earth [the birth of Christ], the greater was the deficit in true and holy guides, the more numerous were the false teachers; from the early beginnings of the printing press, the earth was flooded, like the apocalyptic waters, from which many people died a spiritual death. "Many false prophets will rise up and deceive many" (Matt 24:11). This prophecy has come to pass: its harvest is before our eyes. And there is another prophecy about the character of our times in which will be His second and terrible coming on Earth. When "the Son of Man" said the Lord, pointing to the future of faith, "comes, will He really find faith on the earth?" (Luke 18:8). Then the earth will be dominated by false reason, human wisdom of man, hostile to faith and God alike.

What does it mean to be pious as a monastic: obedience? This piety recognizes that human reasoning is in a fallen state and therefore needs to be rejected by a mighty battle through faith. From faith comes obedience; from obedience comes humility; from humility comes a spiritual mind, which is an informed faith. Monastic obedience was flowering when there were plenty of spiritual leaders. With the disappearance of God-bearing spiritual leaders, the great spiritual struggle of obedience that accelerated the monastic's journey to sainthood also practically disappeared. Faith, which is the heart of this spiritual struggle, demands that the person be a true and spiritual subject: then it leads him to God. Faith in humans leads to uncontrollable fanaticism. On the other hand, guidance by the writings of the Holy Fathers leads one more slowly, takes one on a journey that gives more occasions to stumble: it is a book sketched on paper, and cannot replace the living book of an individual person.

The mind and heart, charted by the Holy Spirit, is a wondrous book! That is how life gushes from it. That is how life flows to those who listen with faith. The writings of the Holy Fathers became the only handbook for salvation now that spiritual leaders are in such a short supply. Whoever submits to this guide can already be counted among the saved. He who is guided by his own reason, or the teachings of false teachers, can be considered as lost. As an example of how the Holy Fathers consider this topic, I quote from the compositions of Saints Kallistos and Ignatius: "What became for us the reason of our sorrow and lifelessness, considering that we were not created this way? What, on the other hand, became the reason for our renewal and immortality? We found that the reason for the former, that is our decay, was our self-reliance, the arrogance and disobedience of the first Adam, which led to his rejection and crime against God's commandments; the reason for the latter, that is immortality, was the obedience of the second Adam, our Saviour and God Jesus Christ to the Father." "For I have not spoken on My own authority; but the Father who sent Me gave Me a command, what I should say and what I should speak," says the Saviour (John 12:49). As in our forefather and his tribe the root and mother of all sorrows was self-elevation; and in the new man—the God-man Jesus Christ and those who wish to live in imitation of him—the beginning and source of all goodness is humility. We see that this standing and order of things is observed by those who are above us, the saintly hierarchs, the angels given to see God: thus our earthly Church protects them. Contrary to this, we learn and believe that those who turn away from this statute and arrogantly determine to lead a life that is self-willed and disobedient become cut off from God, from the light-filled heavenly heritage, become cut off from the congregational apostolic Church and are sent into the gloom and fire of Gehenna. We maintain that those who were subject to the latter were people who became inspired by the words of crafty agents of the devil, evil-tongued heretics, who due to their self-serving interests and pride were deprived of God's glory and delights, were cast out from the sacred gathering.

The text from which I borrowed the last quotation, the saints themselves complete: "We write this, confirming that sayings of the Fathers, the sayings of the Holy Spirit, as on the columns of the immutable" (*The Philokalia* Part 2, Sts Kallistos and Ignatius, "About silence and prayer," chapter 13).

Having learned the journey to salvation, do not hesitate to walk this road. Conclude this blessed covenant, this union with the holy Truth; commit in your soul to remain faithful to the Truth in your life. From this single blessed intent you will receive a stream of lightness, joy, and strength into your heart, a witness to your acceptance of the holy Truth.

"For with the heart one believes unto righteousness, and with the mouth confession is made unto salvation" (Rom 10:10).[121]

∽ Martyrdom ∽

Your wish to put yourself under complete obedience to an experienced mentor is of no avail. This spiritual struggle is not given for our times. It is not found in the world among Christians, not even in the monasteries. The mortification of one's mind and will cannot be done among worldly people even when they are kind and pious. A spirit-bearing father is needed for that. Only a spirit-bearing person can detect the soul of another person. Only he can discern whence and in what direction the movements of the soul are heading under his direction. For the purity of his conscience the student needs to confess his thoughts with precision and in great detail. The mentor must not use this confession to judge the spiritual condition of the student's soul. The mentor needs to penetrate the condition of the soul using his ascetic sensitivity, taking measure of the student's mind, informing the student of the invisible aspects of his soul. That is how it was done by Pachomius the Great, Theodore the Illumined, and similar saintly mentors of monastics. His followers would ask Theodore the great: "Father—reprove me," and he, moved by the Holy Spirit, revealed to each his innermost ailments of the soul. These outstanding Fathers recognized obedience of monastics as a special gift of the Holy Spirit: that is what a contemporary writer reports, the venerable Cassian. Obedience is a "miracle of faith"! It can be accomplished by God alone. And this was accomplished by those individuals to whom this gift was given from above. But when people wish to reach this goal with their own efforts, by what is usually given by God, then their work is done in vain with futility. Then they are like those mentioned in the Gospels who aimed to build a tower without the means of completing it. All passersby, that is, the demons and passions, laugh at the builders, because superficially they appear to be doing a good deed, but in reality, they are in a deep deception, spiritual blindness, and self-delusion, subjects of their own passions, performing the will of the demons. Many thought to go through this obedience but actually found themselves engaged in their own whimsies, were overzealous in their enthusiasm. Happy is he who has time to shed a tear of repentance in his old age for the diversions of his youth. The Lord spoke about blind mentors and those who chose to follow them: "They are blind leaders of the blind. And if the blind leads the blind, both will fall into the ditch" (Matt 15:14).

A different spiritual struggle is given for our times, linked with many difficulties and much stumbling. We were given a journey that is accomplished not in the clear light of day but at night by the pale light of the moon and stars. For our guidance we are given the sacred and Holy Scriptures: the Holy Fathers of the later times speak directly to us. Together with the guidance of the Scriptures it is beneficial to have the advice of those close by, specifically those who themselves were guided by the Scriptures. Do not think our spiritual struggle will lack sorrows and martyr's crowns: no! It is linked with martyrdom. This martyrdom is like the languor of Lot in Sodom: the soul of the righteous languished before the sight of endless and uncontrollable fornication. And we languish, surrounded everywhere by minds of those who violated truth, those who are in a prodigal bond with deception, infected by their hatred for the Scriptures that are inspired by God, armed with blasphemy, slander, and hellish mocking. Our spiritual struggle has value before God: for His scales weigh our debility, our means, our circumstances, and our very time. A certain great Father had this vision: before him our earthly life appeared as a sea. He saw that the ascetics of olden times of monasticism were given fiery wings and they were carried over the sea of passions with ease. The ascetics of recent times were not given wings; they began to cry at the edge of the sea. Then they were given wings, but not fiery ones, rather weak ones; they were carried across the sea. Along the way, because of the weak condition of the wings, they often sank into the sea; with great difficulty they rose from the sea, resumed their flight, and sank again into the sea; with great difficulty and many attempts they finally made it across to the safety of the other shore.

Let us not despair! Let us not irrationally aim for brilliant goals, which exaggerate our strength; let us take upon ourselves a humble and meek goal, appropriate to our weakened state, given to us apparently by the hand of God. Let us complete this goal faithfully amidst the world, among the noise, countless crowds straining along the wide path in pursuit of self-willed rationalism, while we travel the narrow path of obedience to the Church and the Holy Fathers. Not many travel along this path? What of it! The Saviour said, "Do not fear, little flock, for it is your Father's good pleasure to give you the kingdom" (Luke 12:32). "Enter by the narrow gate; for wide is the gate and broad is the way that leads to destruction, and there are many who go in by it. Because narrow is the gate and difficult is the way which leads to life, and there are few who find it" (Matt 7:13–14).[122]

~ Reading ~

You ask why it is necessary to read the writings of the Holy Fathers! Is it not enough to read the Word of God, being guided by Holy Scripture alone, the pure Word of God, which has no impure additives from human writing?

I answer: certainly when reading scripture, one needs to also read the Fathers of the Eastern Church. This is what St Peter the apostle says about Scripture: "All prophecy found in books does not exist by its word alone." "No prophecy of Scripture is of any private interpretation, for prophecy never came by the will of man, but holy men of God spoke as they were moved by the Holy Spirit" (2 Pet 1:20–21). Why then do you arbitrarily wish to comprehend the holy words, which were not uttered randomly but by the urging of the Holy Spirit? The Spirit uttered Holy Scripture, and only the Spirit can interpret it. Men who are inspired by God, the Holy Fathers interpreted it. Therefore, any one wishing to acquire a true knowledge of Holy Scripture must read the Holy Fathers. If you limit yourself to the reading of Holy Scripture, this necessarily will force you to understand and explain it arbitrarily. By the same necessity you will not be able to avoid delusions, because "natural man does not receive the things of the Spirit of God, for they are foolishness to him; nor can he know them, because they are spiritually discerned" (1 Cor 2:14). "No one knows the things of God except the Spirit of God" (1 Cor 2:11).

Heretics of all times especially hate Scripture commentary of the Fathers: writings of the Fathers reveal the meaning of Scriptures directly, while the enemies of Truth would have liked to distort the Truth in order to reinforce their false reasoning. Heresiarch Eftichios expressed his averseness to the Fathers at the local council in Constantinople. "Holy Scripture," he said slyly, "must be more respected than the writings of the fathers," because the writings of the holy patriarchs of Alexandria Athanasius the Great and recently reposed Cyril clearly denounced his delusions as blasphemous. The Universal Church, on the contrary, always cherished a special respect for

Patristic Scriptures: thanks to the Scriptures, the unity of the church was preserved by all and the truthful, blessed interpretation of the Scriptures. The Universal Councils were always begun with readings from the Fathers' Scriptures, in which dogmatics and tradition were outlined in special detail and whose review was the object and reason for the council meeting. Relying on the Scriptures of the Fathers, the council denounced the heresy, announcing the Orthodox teachings and faith. Exactly the same way in their private life, the holy ascetics would be instructed in the Scriptures of the Fathers and only then would they graduate to reading mostly Holy Scripture, after reaching a certain spiritual maturity. St John of the Ladder said: "Deep is the sea of Scripture, and the mind of the hesychast travels on the sea not without danger: it is dangerous to swim clothed, and touch holy writ by one who is full of passions" (Word 27, about silence). This danger, this disaster, apparently, lies in arbitrary reasoning, in a false understanding of Scriptures, and why many monastics fell into a fatal delusion. In vain do heretics demonstrate their alleged respect for the Holy Scriptures false, hypocritical: that of respect for the word of God as though it is presented to everyone no matter how flawed, to interpret it arbitrarily. The Holy Church accepts the interpretation of Holy Scripture by the Holy Fathers, thereby proving its deep respect for the Scripture. She teaches its children not to be arrogant in regard to the Word of God, holds them back from proud self-rule and lack of respect, brings them up reading the commandments, and instructs them to study the marvelous light of God's word, and under guidance allows them to look upon this light, strikes blind those who dare look upon the word of God without proper preparation, with unclean minds and impure hearts. It is worthwhile to pay attention to the liturgy of the Eastern Church, to reassure oneself of the great respect shown to the Scriptures. The Gospel is the all-holy book that contains the words spoken to man by God incarnate Himself, and it can always be found on the holy altar, clearly representing Christ Himself. During all public readings, it is removed from the altar, preceded by lighted candles. It is carried out and placed on the stand in the middle of the church; then all Orthodox Christians present reverently bend their knees before the Holy Scriptures as before the word of God. With fear and love they approach to kiss the holy book. Meanwhile the heretic, having just praised his own respect for Holy Scriptures, dares to mock the children of the church before the Gospel of Christ, calling them idolatrous worshippers of paper, ink, and book binding: wretched blind man! He sees in that Book only paper, ink, and binding. He does not see the Gospel of Christ. Public reading of the Apostles is performed by the deacon and readers; the latter do their reading aloud in the middle of the church. Liturgical songs, composed by Holy Fathers, contain the full course of dogmatic and moral teaching of theology. Glory to God for preserving His Church in purity and sacredness! Glory to the holy Eastern Church, the only holy and true one! All her heritage, all her customs are sacred, containing the spiritual fragrance and anointment! May all the heretical movements be ashamed, all who seek to sever its unity.

Have reverence for Holy Scriptures, reverence due to the real Son of the true Church; have proper veneration for the same patristic writings. The same Spirit of God who acted through the prophets and apostles also acted upon the holy pastors and teachers of the Church: the witness to this is the holy apostle: "God has appointed these in the church: first apostles, second prophets, third teachers" (1 Cor 12:28). Consistent with the words of the apostle, according to Holy Scripture, the primary place in our readings should be given to the readings from the Apostles. Among the writings of the Apostles, readings from the Gospels take first place. In order to correctly understand the New Testament, read the holy teachers of the Church, read the Psalms and other books of the Old Testament. Purify yourself with commandments from the Gospels and pious struggles. In accordance with the purity of the soul, God appears there, and the word of God is revealed to the soul, but for carnal eyes these things are inaccessible, being blocked by the curtain of the word of man.[123]

∽ Love ∽

The New Testament decrees we should love our enemies: the Holy Fathers applaud love for all people. Why should the love of one's neighbors not be distinguished from any other kind of love?

This is what I'd like to discuss with you now. I'd like to give you these words not from myself but from God: the merciful God gives me these words. I recognize only that love that acts according to the holy decrees of the New Testament, under its illumination, whose light is itself love. No other love do I understand, nor accept. The love that is extolled by the world, recognized by people as their possession, marked by the fall, is unworthy of being called love: that love is a distortion of holy and true love. That is why it bears such enmity to holy and true love.

True, holy love of God and one's neighbor is precisely described in New Testament commandments; the correct, unblemished actions of this love are to be found in the carrying out of New Testament commandments. "He who loves me," said the Lord, "has my commandments and keeps them" (John 14:21). Such love can have no dreaminess, no carnal heat, because the rendition of Christ's commandments is achieved by beginners through force against oneself, with such force that it is called crucifixion, and those who prosper in this experience a blessed illumination and receive abundant sensations of Christ's peace. The peace of Christ is a certain refined spiritual coolness: when it flows over your soul it abides in a high state of silence, in a sacred stillness of death.

"Do not think that I came," says the Lawgiver of holy and true love, says Love itself—God, "to bring peace on earth. I did not come to bring peace but a sword. For I have come to set a man against his father, a daughter against her mother, and a daughter-in-law against her mother-in-law; and a man's enemies will be those of his own household" (Matt 10:34–36). And all our deeds concerning our neighbor, both good and evil, the Lord will judge, as though they were done against Himself (Matt 25). The entire doctrine the Lord distilled into two commandments: love of God and love of one's neighbor. "Love . . . is the bond of perfection" (Col 3:14), said the Apostle. If that is so, then why the sword and why enmity and separation? Because God rejects carnal love, the love that Adam learned after the fall. He acccpts only one spiritual love, the one revealed by the New Adam, our Lord Jesus Christ. We need to love as He loves: love of the fallen Adam of old is a fruit forbidden in the heaven of the New Testament. That kind of love proceeds from reverie, changeability, bias, it loves creatures apart from God. God is removed completely from participating in this love, sin and Satan are designed to participate in this love.

Spiritual love is constant, unbiased, it abides completely in God, embraces all neighbors, loves all equally, but with a big difference. "Love your enemies," says the New Testament, "bless those who curse you, do good to those who hate you, and pray for those who spitefully use you and persecute you" (Matt 5:44). Here is a clear and definite exposition how we must love our enemies, how to forgive them for the offenses they brought upon us, how to pray for them, how to use blessed words over them, how to thank God for the blows brought down on us by our enemies, how to thank them according to our strength and spiritual condition even unto death for the salvation of our enemy. An example of that kind of love for the enemy was given us by our Saviour.

The very same New Testament commands us to take precautions with our enemies and not entrust ourselves to them. "Behold I send you out," the Lord said to his disciples, "as sheep in the midst of wolves. Therefore be wise as serpents and harmless as doves. But beware of men, for they will deliver you up to councils and scourge you in their synagogues. . . . You will be hated by all for My name's sake" (Matt 10:16–17, 22). And so the New Testament itself instructs us to be careful of our enemies, and whenever possible, conduct ourselves wisely with them. The spirit of the world [Satan that is] creates hostility, which sometimes takes the place of carnal love. And carnal love itself resembles hostile relations. One of Adam's descendants experienced love and hostility: the closer he resembled his ancient relative, the stronger were his afflictions, with which he destroyed love: hostility, envy, jealousy, carnal love. The Servant of God cannot be an enemy toward anyone.

The New Testament assigns us to love our enemies not blindly, not unreasonably, but sanctified with spiritual reason. Love is light, a blind love is not love. Similarly, we need to speak about the love of our friends. The New Testament instructs that this love be about Christ, that Christ be loved in the person of our neighbor, and that the neighbor be loved as a creature of God. By virtue of this love of God and for the sake of God, the holy saints also had an equal love for all and loved especially those who led worthy lives, as holy David explained: "But Thy friends, have been very dear to me, O God; their powers have been greatly strengthened" (Ps 138:17 LXX). Those being led were more inclined to those teachers in whom they saw plenty of spiritual gifts. And the teachers loved those spiritual children of theirs in whom they observed a spirit of goodwill toward a virtuous life and noticed signs of God's mercy. Such love brought a measure of virtue to people according to their degree of piety; at the same time it was equally attentive to everyone, because this love was founded on the love of Christ. One vessel holds more of this spiritual treasure, another less so. The treasure is the same!

Where there is Christ, there is no envy or eagerness. "Love . . . thinks no evil" (1 Cor 13:5). There we find calm and a holy peace. Love that is accompanied by eagerness is earthly, physical, and unclean. The eyes of holy love are like an eagle's, like the eyes of a flaming Cherubim: even the tiniest sinful movement cannot hide from them. This holy love is inaccessible to sin, which is always bound to the earth; holy love resides in Heaven to which the heart and mind are transported, being collaborators of the love of God.[124]

∼ Health ∼

Remember, my most honorable benefactor, that our Lawgiver suffered on the Cross and informed both his followers and servants: "In the world you will have tribulation" (John 16:33). Why tribulations? Because the world will hate you, and my own Father "every branch in Me that does not bear fruit He takes away; and every branch that bears fruit He prunes, that it may bear more fruit" (John 15:2). And so, be of good cheer amidst the unrest, surrender yourself to the will of God, with joy and gratitude release your illness, knowing that physical illnesses heal the soul. Repeat as often as possible the following prayer: *Lord, may Your will be done!* It is brief, however it contains broad significance and has a powerful ability to calm the person, who finds himself in trouble. I discovered this partially through my own experience. But why cite one's worthless experience, when the Saviour of this World Himself spoke this holy prayer in the vineyard and barred with this prayer any petitions that might have issued from human weakness.

I hope in the mercy of the Lord and await that happy hour when I shall see you face to face. May the Lord return to you your good health, so that your physical strength is plentiful and may every happiness be aplenty with you in your good works in the name of our Lord Jesus Christ and for the Church in general and certainly for her true members.[125]

～ Death ～

You are a guardian of the poor, with your faith you often bring the rich from their place of corruption into the bosom of Abraham. From your image as a younger brother of Christ, He Himself will receive your wards and your service, just as he would receive them from the servants of the Church. Your outward appearance is not as brilliant, but your essence is the same O! How many glorious services, which tempt one with ambition, engage and inflame our imagination: but the end crowns the work. Death comes, calls to a life without ghosts; and to this invitation, no matter how bitter it may be, no one can refuse. Tsars depart, without completing enormous plans, whose fulfillment could benefit millions of people; geniuses depart, abandoning what was begun for the delight of the next generation; lawmakers depart without completing their legislative works; in one instant marks of distinction and loud titles are set aside, which required an entire lifetime to achieve. Those rich in faith, by contrast, become even richer, for by death they enter into substantial possession of what before death they only believed in through faith.[126]

∼ Perfection ∼

The difference between people in the world and in monasteries is not adequately explained, so clearly revealed from the words of our Saviour to the young man: "If you want to enter into life, keep the commandments. . . . 'You shall not murder,' 'You shall not commit adultery,' 'You shall not steal,' 'You shall not bear false witness'" (Matt 19:16–21). This is the action of the person living in the world, whose purpose is to be saved. To the question posed by the youth, which he did not finish, the Saviour teaches that in Christian life there can be perfection; who wishes to be perfect must first leave all things of the world and then naked, bereft of everything, take up the labor of reaching perfection. This is reflected in the parable in which the Kingdom of Heaven is likened to the merchant, who discovers that in a certain village a treasure is hidden, and he sells all his belongings in order to buy the village, and not the treasure. Saint Macarius of Egypt said, he who distributed all his belongings, and left all the pleasures of the world, went into a monastery, and has still not accomplished anything, only became naked in order to step into a new field. We do not know if he will reach his goal.

Christian perfection consists in acquiring a pure heart, to which God comes and takes residence by means of many kinds of gifts of the Holy Spirit. He who reaches such perfection becomes a lamp, not by his physical labors but through the Holy Spirit who fulfills the commandment to love one's neighbor, as a guide for saving others, saving them from falling, healing the wounds of their soul. The monastic image gave the Church of Christ priests who did not spar using human wisdom but guided their flock using words of the Holy Spirit, accompanying their teaching with miracles, shepherded their flock, and reinforced the Church. That is why at the end of the martyrdoms the Church is seen as fleeing into monasteries. The perfection of the Church was fleeing there, the source of holy light, the main strength of the Church militant. Who were Chrysostom, Basil the Great, Epiphanios, Metropolitans Alexii and Philip, in one word, all holy pastors? But not under the rank of archbishop, but under the unassuming mantle of a monk there are many beacons of spirituality from Anthony the Great and John of Damascus to Sergius of Radonezh and George the recluse. They lay the foundations of faith, denounced the heresies and trampled them. Without monastics, faith among those living in the world would disappear. That is why the Church of Christ needs perfection, without which salvation and faith itself could be lost, and lost they would certainly be, because we need sensitivity developed over a long period of time to help us differentiate between good and evil (Heb 5:14). This perfection was achieved during the early Christian church by ascetics and martyrs and later by monastics. Chastity, poverty, labor, vigilance, active love: these are the tools and means for achieving perfection but not the ultimate perfection. It appears that in the letter this is mentioned unclearly, that is why the distinguishing features of monasticism are not presented in their full force. It would benefit the writer of this letter to read the discourses of Macarius of Egypt in order to reinforce his words with spiritual concepts. People will say: what a proud assessment of monasticism, denouncing the pride of the heart. We respond: in a dark room it is hard to notice significant dirt; however, in a room illuminated by bright rays of the sun even light dust is visible and disturbs the owner. The Holy Spirit is the teacher of humility; having inhabited the heart, it sighs with exclamations unspoken and shows man the worthlessness of his righteousness, as Isaiah speaks: "All our righteousness is like a filthy rag" (Isa 64:5 LXX). Real demonic pride rejects the gift of God as though it did not exist.[127]

∿ Illness ∿

St Isaac the Syrian rightfully says: there is no more precious topic in the world than the love of one's neighbor, through which we enter into the love of God. Perhaps I overdid my writing exercises to excess, or my weak physical constitution was affected by temptations, or my chronic illness, tapeworm. All these things brought me by the middle of winter into such a sickly state that I stopped eating, felt a most powerful pain in my chest. During Great Lent I was so very weak that I barely signed my name on the lectern; and since Passion Week I have been getting better. I spend my time as usual: sorting through monastic books of the Holy Fathers, among which God helped me finish the translation from Latin of the book of Saint Isaiah the recluse. I hope you will read this book for your own spiritual benefit and delight, for you have a taste for profound sensations, born from humility that arises from interior contemplation of man. God grant that all of us be saved from snakes—that is, our passions, which are assisted by those other serpents, the demons.[128]

∿ Humility ∿

St Isaiah [the Recluse]. From his Word VIII. If you have lent something to your neighbor and do not ask for it back, then you are imitating the nature of Christ; and if you ask for it back, then you are imitating the nature of Adam: if you demand more [than what you lent], then this is lower than the nature of Adam. If someone reproaches you for something you did or did not do, and you will stay silent, then you become like Christ; if you will respond, protesting, what have I done? Then you are not like Christ anymore; if you respond in kind then you are not at all like Him. If you bring your offering with humility, as one who is unworthy, then it will be received favorably by God. If you become proud in your heart and think of others who are lazy or slothful, then your labor will be in vain. Humility does not even have a tongue to speak about those who are slothful or careless; does not have eyes to see the sins of others; does not have ears to hear that which cannot bring profit to the soul; finally, it has no cares except to care about its own sins. The humble person is concerned with preserving peace, not for the sake of friendship but for the sake of the commandments of God.

St Isaiah. Word XVII. Whoever tramples on his conscience chases away virtues from his heart. Whoever fears God is diligent, whoever does not fear God falls victim to negligence. Whoever guards his lips and stays silent wisely elevates his thoughts to God. Wordiness breeds laziness and rage. He who defers to the will of his neighbor discovers the soul is diligent in finding virtues; on the other hand, he who is adamant about following his will discovers his own ignorance. Fear of God and secret teaching guard the heart from passions. Worldly chatter subjects the heart to gloom and turns it away from virtues. The mind and heart become perturbed by love of earthly things, disdain for these things brings silence and calm. Rust eats away at steel; similarly ambition eats away at the human heart. Ivy, which winds itself around a grape vine, destroys the fruit of the vine; in a similar fashion ambition subverts the works of man. Humility underlies all virtues, and gluttony underlies all passions. The object of virtues is love, and the object of passions is considering oneself the most righteous.

Conclusion of St Isaiah. Word XVII. Brothers! Let us make the effort, while we are still in our flesh, to fill our vessels with oil, so that our lamp would give light, when we enter the Kingdom. A light and brilliant lamp is our holy soul. For the soul, bright with our good deeds, will enter the Kingdom, while the soul, darkened by evil, will descend into the gloom. And so, be courageous, brothers, be diligent with your good deeds, for time is nigh. Blessed is he who takes strict account of himself. The wheat has ripened and ready for harvest. Blessed is he who keeps his harvest, and the angels will come, and take the harvest into the eternal barn. Woe be to those who lose heart, for fire awaits them. The legacy of this world is gold and silver, and homes, and cloth-ing: all of these give cause for sinfulness, and with all this we must part when we enter the next world. The legacy that God brings is measure-less, the "eye has not seen, nor the ear heard, nor have entered into the heart of man the things which God has prepared for those that love Him" (1 Cor 2:9). This legacy is given to those who in the short space of their life submit to the commandments of the Lord. It is given for the bread, for the water, for the clothing which we give to the poor, for the love of man, for chastity of the body, for an incorrupt heart, and other virtues.[129]

∼ Health ∼

I cannot participate in the secular celebrations of my family; how-ever, I do wish to take an active part in their struggles. One elects to go into the monastery so that a life of pleasure does not lead to a forgetfulness of God, so that with vanity one does not leave what is legitimate and holy. I am convinced from the word of God and my own life experience that those whom God loves, He is sure to send trials. Because without afflictions of the heart one cannot mortify things of this world and live for God in eternity. Hearing that you are constantly ailing, I understood that the Lord took special notice of you and wishes to give you a blissful eternity. We must all certainly enter into eternity and those of us who do not want to consider any of this in our thoughts or wishes must always be nailed to everything of this world. Eternity! With what joyful hope some wait for eternity and how formidable it is for others. And so, if eternity awaits all of us certainly, then reason demands that we prepare for it with prudence. Therefore, I advise you, regarding your health, to rely on the will of God. Keep in mind the thought that God is calling you to Himself, with your tribulations, thank your Creator, who has loved you and repeat often these words: Glory to Thee, Lord, for everything that you are sending me. Do Your will onto Your servant. Thanksgiv-ing for afflictions brings patience and strength to endure all. Do not wish for death. God does not send it, so that we are not prepared for it, as something expected. As much as you endure in this life with thanksgiving, that much more will you enjoy spiritual delight in the next life.[130]

∽ Sufferings ∽

May the Lord sustain you in your affliction! Please accept my own sinful and inadequate word of comfort that I send you in these lines, in order to comfort you with God, as the prophet David said: "I remembered God, and I was glad; I mused, and my spirit faltered" (Ps 76:4 LXX). First of all, each Christian must believe that he is under unceasing Divine Providence. The Gospel teaches this to us. The Saviour Himself says: "But the very hairs of your head are all numbered" (Luke 12:7). Therefore, Christian, when afflictions are permitted to overcome you, you must certainly believe that these afflictions are permitted by God, Who foretold to those He loved: "In the world you will have tribulation" (John 16:33). Thus do not consider it strange, seeing yourself in afflictions, do not indulge in despair; on the contrary, thank God for your troubles, as a sign of being chosen for a blessed eternity. Thanksgiving not only dulls the sting of sorrow, but your grateful heart receives a heavenly, spiritual comfort. You can say thanks with the words of righteous Job.

Secondly, we are all sinners before God. The sinner should not think it strange when he is sent chastisement. No! He should be open before God, acknowledge himself worthy of the sorrow sent, and rejoice that he received punishment in his earthly life for sins committed in full knowledge of ignorance and thus avoided eternal torment [in the next world after death]. With such thinking it is useful to say with the holy thief "we receive the due reward of our deeds" (Luke 23:41). "Lord, remember me when You come into Your kingdom" (Luke 23:42).

Christ completed His earthly sojourn in constant sorrows. No sooner was He born than people already aimed to kill Him. He invites His apostles to suffer with Him and to those who do not wish to suffer He says: "And whoever does not bear his cross and come after Me cannot be My disciple" (Luke 14:27). Consider the life of all the apostles: all spent and finished their lives in suffering. Consider the lives of martyrs: they purchased their heaven with their blood and countless suffering. Consider the lives of venerable monks: was not their whole life a continuous invisible martyrdom? They wandered in remote monasteries, inhabited solitary dens and caverns, experienced deprivation, afflictions, bitterness of the world, according to apostles' words "by means of much blood and dying" they won themselves a blessed eternity. "No one will ascend to heaven with less, said the saint, the great Isaac the Syrian, on the contrary, thus is a man marked who find himself under special Providence of God, when he is sent ceaseless sorrows." So, give thanks, be humble, believe, submit to the will of God. Only in this will you find comfort and healing.[131]

∼ Trials ∼

I heartily wish you physical and spiritual health. May you have strength from our All-blessed Lord and Jesus Christ who redeemed us with his precious Blood; may He give you patience in your ailments and other sorrows and inspire you to give thanks for them, as for the greatest of blessings. Hear His holy voice, announcing, "As many as I love, I rebuke and chasten" (Rev 3:19). Remember the righteous Job, deprived of his children and all his goods, covered in stinking sores, sitting among mounds of pus and saying, "The Lord gave, and the Lord has taken away . . . Blessed be the name of the Lord" (Job 1:21). Remember the prophet Jonah from the belly of the whale declaring his sins and glorifying the justice of God. Remember the three young men cast into the fiery furnace and glorifying God from the depth of the furnace. Remember all the saints and the journey by which they gained salvation. Did they not take the narrow and sorrowful path into the heart of their life? Remember all this and envy the lot of the saints, tell your cowardly thoughts: all hairs on my head are accounted for by God, how can you despair? "God is faithful, who will not allow you to be tempted beyond what you are able, but with the temptation will also make the way of escape" (1 Cor 10:13). Let us thank our merciful God for everything, and let us pray to Him, to preserve us in love and harmony for the glory of His holy name.[132]

∼ Eternity ∼

Exactly, life on earth is full of sorrows; when a person completes a significant part of his life and looks back, then it seems all that was pleasant was actually vain that for which he was yearning with such hunger in his youth! Let us then not lose at least the rest of our life by sacrificing it in hectic pursuit of all that is vain. Let us get acquainted with eternity not by reading little foreign books, which lead the reader invariably to self-deception. Instead be guided by the holy writers of our Church, where there is nothing romantic, dreamy, or flattering in garnering knowledge about our relationship to God, our Creator and Redeemer, where we are taught to approach Him with repentance, where we are not flattered with imaginary sweet emotions about spiritual love, to which are attracted the extravagant likes of Thomas a Kempis, Francois de Sales, and other false teachers. Spiritual love is the reward of those who reach perfection; and the reward of the righteous and those who fear God, those who see their own sins and shortcomings; the product of one and the other is a contrite and humble heart, which expresses repentance. This is the true moral teaching of the Orthodox Church, to which any kind of deception and self-delusion is foreign. I invoke God's blessing upon you and feelings of heartfelt devotion, with wishes for all good things for you, especially for true soulful Christian edification, which is the highest blessing on earth and a token of our blessings in heaven.[133]

∼ Health ∼

Time of afflictions, a time for patience! Afflictions are allowed by God and need to be tolerated with obedience and reverence, giving credit to the most just God and considering oneself deserving of them. From such a position of our soul, we can pray to God for mercy in the hope of being heard. Such an acceptance of God's justice with a prayer for mercy is excellently described in the prayer of the three holy young men of Judah, who were plunged into the fiery furnace of Babel. This prayer is found in the book of Daniel. I would be ashamed to write about patience with afflictions if I did not find myself in them. From the second week of Great Lent I became very ill. Repeatedly I felt such weakness, as if I were dying, and now feel very poorly. I do not quite know how to thank God for bringing me out of mundane life and leading me into the monastery! At an early age one feels that life is a boundless field of activity and when a person finishes it and looks back, one invariably sees in the activities lived through much emptiness. Affliction increasingly takes on the character of public life. And here one expects an increase in the price of bread, thanks to a reduction in the number of crops being planted. May the blessings of God rest upon you and upon your sons.[134]

∼ Health ∼

Old people used to say: may the Lord allow me to suffer well before dying. Niphont the Great, dying of a fever, told Athanasius the Great, who was present at his death, that just like gold is purified by fire, so the dying one is purified by illness. The eyes of the dying person's soul are opened and that is why they see what those who are present at their death cannot see. The Light that you write about was from heaven. Apparently: Semion was blessed by the grace of God. Talk to his children, tell them to give alms to the poor in abundance in honor of their father. Giving alms helps the departed a great deal, and God will bless the children for this, and their conscience will be more at peace. You did well to remove any embarrassment from the dying man. And now calm down and leave everything to God. "To his own master he stands or falls," said the Apostle Paul (Rom 14:4).

I believe, not without the Providence of God, were you present at this death that was accompanied with such suffering. This death will stay in your memory and such remembrance will serve to prepare you for your own death. For because you served your brother, the merciful Lord will reward you with a spiritual gift that only He knows about. Try to calm yourself, and submit to the will of God.[135]

～ Afflictions ～

The Holy Fathers advise us to thank God for afflictions given us and tell us to confess in our prayers that we are worthy of the punishment sent to us for our sins. Thus, by accepting our struggles, they will serve to cleanse us of our sins and become a pledge toward our eternal bliss. By virtue of our fallen nature we care more about arranging our temporary comfort on this earth, while God arranges for our eternal destiny, about which we would have forgotten if our earthly lot would not have been shaken by struggles, if afflictions sent to us from time to time by God's Providence did not remind us that all earthly things pass away and that our main concern should be eternity. Holy Scripture says: "For whom the Lord loves He chastens" (Heb 12:6). God sends chastening afflictions to those whom He takes mercy upon, but to those who have rejected Him, He sends final and crushing sorrows such as sudden death and deprivation of sanity and such. Great is our God! A terrible thing is the fall of man! A great deed is the redemption of man through God Who became Man! It is essential to thoroughly study all this and correctly understand about God and oneself in order to guide our earthly wanderings in order not to be lost forever.[136]

〜 Afflictions 〜

God, who governs all things, is especially heedful of those people, who wish to serve Him, and are beset by afflictions. He takes them by the thorny path, wresting them from the world by sorrows that lead them to Him. Then He saves them from all sorrows, so that their mature sight allows them to see His Divine Providence and acquire faith in Him. We need to be mindful of death, whose memory sobers us by not knowing the hour and formidable torment that awaits every person after death. However, it is also necessary to know that by the assurance of the Holy Fathers, sudden death does not happen to people who wish to purify themselves with repentance, even though they were defeated at times by afflictions; the righteous and merciful God will give them an end, which is commensurate with their intentions.[137]

〜 Afflictions 〜

Regarding the stumbling blocks for a Christian who by the inscrutable ways of God is still living in the world, the following was written by the Holy Fathers, which is worth repeating. A Christian is like a ship, and Christian life among other men in the world is like sailing in a ship on the sea. The ship, as long as it is at sea, is subject to the effects of winds, currents, stormy waves, is in danger of striking underwater rocks or other ships, is exposed to manifold dangers, suffers from multiple damage, all of which is healed by repentance. When a ship docks, there is other danger; the ship master unloads the goods that filled the ship, creating trade with which big profits are made. It is not possible when on the open sea to claim the peace that is found in a safe harbor. It is not possible to manufacture goods on the open sea. Once more, it is impossible for a ship to enter the shelter of a calm harbor without first undergoing the arduous journey on the high seas. Similarly, until a man lives among other men and experiences the misfortunes arising in the world and as a result of his own fall, God cannot lead him to a calm and safe harbor. Only God knows how much a man must live among the waves and storms of the sea of life and when to lead him into the quiet harbor by waves of repentance. But abundant fruit is collected in solitude and is the product of much struggle after life among people. The latter is the foundation for the first. That is why those who wish to earn sinless salvation must submit themselves to the all-holy will of God and pray to God to grant them salvation. Salvation is not a human undertaking, or the business of man, but is the work of God and a gift of God to man.[138]

∼ Mercy ∼

I have told you about the need to sever your will. This refers specifically to your ascetic struggle in prayer. You must renounce in yourself any feeling of worthiness in your efforts and acquire poverty of spirit (which is the same renouncing of your will). You must heed the words and your fear of God while standing mentally before Him, with heartfelt crying for mercy and expect everything from His mercy. He will deal with us according to His will and according to His mercy: then it will become evident that the benefits God conferred upon you are quite different from what man supposed to receive. Those who have not cut off their will are in danger of self-delusion. I am telling you what is essential for you.

Who should support the church? To do this, people of grace are needed, while worldly reasoning is only capable of doing damage and destruction. Although reason in all its pride and blindness dreams and proclaims about creation.[139]

∼ Afflictions ∼

I was glad the thought of death came to your mind and that you understand the danger of your illness. The remembrance of death does not bring death closer but only prepares you for it and inclines you to repentance. Your wound and pain from it is a fatherly chastisement from God, for "For whom the Lord loves, He instructs" (Prov 3:12).

I have spent all my life in sickness and afflictions as you know: now however if there were no afflictions, there would be nothing to save us. Heroic struggles are no more, true monasticism is no more, leaders are no more: only afflictions replace everything else. A spiritual struggle is bound with vanity; vanity is difficult to detect in oneself and even more difficult to cleanse oneself of it; sorrow is alien to vanity, that is why it brings to each person blessed involuntary spiritual struggle that is sent by our Providential God according to our volition. At my age and with my sickliness I must seek repentance. Everything will come in due course into the gloom of the grave of oblivion: only service to God and repentance before Him will have any eternal value. It seems the earth is preparing for a great battle, but the combat with passions and lowly desires is completely left behind. A general weakening of faith is very noticeable. Take heart! The Lord will comfort and give you cover with His mercy.[140]

∼ Consolation ∼

God arranged for you to become ill in your old age and to sit in your cell, so you can recall the sins of your youth and through them bring repentance to God and thus receive forgiveness from Him. Thank God, who arranges our salvation by means of His wisdom for our destinies. You must understand from the illness that came to you in your monastic cell that God accepted your decision to enter the monastery and is rewarding you for your compulsive service to Him in the monastery. The apostle says: "For whom the Lord loves He chastens" (Heb 12:6). And so, even though you now feel the beatings, however, they are signs of acceptance and should be received with joy and thanksgiving. From thanksgiving comes patience and a hope of salvation.[141]

∼ Surrender ∼

St John Chrysostom and other Fathers, when beginning to speak about something, would always start with the following words: "May the will of God be with all of us! Thank God for everything being done even though it may be done with difficulty and bitterness." God in His abundant goodness is merciful and in his chastisements is all-merciful. It is the business of every Christian to understand this truth. Often it happens that according to the heedfulness of God we may be deprived of something material and temporary, and in its place we are given something moral, spiritual, and eternal. But people, attached to their material, temporary life, do not understand this when they raise material things to a higher good. Surrendering oneself to the will of God brings calm and comfort to the heart in all afflictions. I say this from my own frequent experience, but am certain that this will be confirmed by each person's experiences, if he adjusts himself to the spirit of the Holy Fathers.[142]

His Grace Bishop Ignatius (Brianchaninov). Mixed media: pen and ink with acrylics and 24K gold leaf on Arches paper by Elena Borowski, 2019. Grayscale image.

Appendix

~ A Chronology of the Life of St Ignatius (Brianchaninov) ~

1807—Dimitry Alexandrovich Brianchaninov was born on February 5, 1807, in the village of Pokrovskoye in the Vologda region of Russia. His parents are Alexander Semenovich and Sofia Afanasievna Brianchaninov, one of the oldest and wealthiest landowning aristocratic families of Russia. Dimitry was the first of sixteen children, only nine of whom survived. He was born during the epoch of Alexander I (1801–25) and lived during the Napoleonic Wars and defeat of Napoleon (1812–14). He lived through the reigns of Nicholas I (1825–55), Alexander II (1855–61), and the first years of Alexander III (1861–94) of Russia. As were his brothers and sisters, he was home-schooled in a highly disciplined household, expected to know court etiquette and be familiar with European culture and languages. In his youth he developed a love for solitude in the peaceful surroundings of his country home.

1822—Being the most gifted of the children, by age 15, Dimitry knew five languages: French, German, English, old Greek, and Latin. His tutor introduced him to the Holy Scriptures and other spiritual readings.

1824—His father brought him to the main military engineering school in St Petersburg. On the way Dimitry humbly expressed his wish for monastic life, which his father firmly rejected. Dimitry did well at the entrance exams and was placed into the second class. While in St Petersburg he had access to the exclusive salons hosted by his relative Alexei N. Olenin, president of the Imperial Academy of the Arts. There Dimitry met the outstanding literary figures of the day: Pushkin, Krylov, Gnedich, and Batiushkov. At these events, Dimitry was applauded for his readings of poetry and essays of his own composition. This was a time in Russian society, especially since Peter the

Great's extensive reforms, when European culture was much admired, while Russian culture and the heritage of Holy Russia was diminished or ignored. Many Russian people moved away from Orthodoxy and the Church. Grand Duke Nicholas Pavlovich, the future Tsar Nicholas I, took special notice of Dimitry, whom he wished to promote to military service. Dimitry's studies at the academy left him cold and spiritually empty. In St Petersburg, with its busy social life and formality, he lost the sweet silence of his youth. He prayed to God to show him a way out of this desolation. He encountered Fr Leonid (the future Optina elder Lev) in the Alexander-Nevsky Lavra but visits to Fr Leonid and the church were blocked by his parents, who feared he was moving toward a monastic life. On his own, Dimitry turned to studying the Early Church Fathers—Anthony the Great, Arseny the Great, Makarius of Egypt—whom he read independently in their own language and began to translate into Russian.

1826—Dimitry completed his studies at the Main Engineering Academy, where he finished at the top of his class. Again he asked his parents' blessings to enter monastic life and was firmly refused. Tsar Nicholas I compelled Dimitry to accept a special assignment in military service, which Dimitry tried unsuccessfully to refuse.

1827—In November Dimitry fell ill making it possible for him to request an honorable discharge. After making a full recovery, he and his school friend, Mikhail Chikhachev, began their wanderings among Russian monasteries in search of an experienced spiritual father and a place to practice ascetic struggles. Dimitry became a novice at the Alexander Svirsky Monastery to which Fr Leonid had moved; however, he found the crowds of pilgrims made solitude impossible. Dimitry had a dream in which St Alexander appeared to him and led him out of the monastery. Fr Leonid understood this to mean that Dimitry would follow a different path of ascetic struggle, and he was released from his noviciate remaining on good terms with Fr Leonid for the rest of his life. Searching for a place to embrace monastic life, he visited the monasteries: Ploshchanskaya *pustyn*, in Orlov Governorat, Optyna

Vvedensky *pustyn*, the Kirillo-Novoyezerskii Monastery, the Semigo-rod *pustyn*, and the Glushitskii Dionysiev Monastery.

1831—On June 28, at the age of 24, in the Vologodsk Cathedral, Dimitry was tonsured as a monk and given the monastic name of Ignatius by Bishop Stefan. His parents ceased all communication and support. His spiritual father was the revered Elder Leonid of Optina.

1831—On July 25, Ignatius was ordained a priest and shortly assigned to build the Pelshemski Lopotov Monastery in the Vologodsk diocese.

1834—Fr Ignatius's absence from the army had come to the attention of Tsar Nicholas, who located him and recalled him to St Petersburg, the capital. At the age of 26, he was made an archimandrite and appointed as abbot of the St Sergius Monastery. His assignment was to revive the monastery that had gone into decline since its founding in 1734 and to make it into a model monastic institution. He labored faithfully there for the next twenty-four years.

1838—Archimandrite Ignatius was assigned Dean of the monasteries in the St Petersburg diocese.

1847—Archimandrite Ignatius's first essay, "A Visit to Valaamski Mon-astery," was published in "Library for Reading." During his life, St Igna-tius was inspired to write both for a monastic audience and for people living in the world. The year 1847 was a time of revolt against European monarchies, beginning in Sicily, spreading to France, Germany, Italy, and the Austrian Empire.

1857—On October 25, Archimandrite Ignatius was ordained to the episcopacy in the Kazan Cathedral (St Petersburg) and served as Bishop of Stavropol and the Caucasus for four years.

1861—On August 5, illness forced Bishop Ignatius to withdraw into seclusion at the Nicolo-Babaevsky Monastery in the Kostroma region of Russia. Finally, he had the solitude and peaceful environment he had been seeking all his adult life. He systematically reread and polished his massive lifelong compositions. Remembering what he learned in his youthful meetings with Pushkin and Gnedich, he went back over everything he had written and devoted these years to correcting and perfecting his spiritual writing and to correspondence with his numerous spiritual children.

1865–67—Bishop Ignatius composed five volumes of *Ascetical Works.*

1867—Bishop Ignatius peacefully fell asleep in the Lord on April 30/ May 13, 1867, the Sunday of the Myrrh-Bearing Women.

1988—The Russian Orthodox Church canonized him at their local council in 1988. His incorrupt relics were moved to the ancient Tolga Monastery on the Volga River in the region of Yaroslavl.

The first publisher of St Ignatius's works in the Russian language was I. Glazunov. Publishing rights to the saint's compositions then passed on to I.K. Tuzov by agreement with the saint's family. Tuzov published the second and third collection of essays in 1886 and 1905.

The fifth volume of his *Ascetical Works* was translated into English by Archimandrite Lazuraus (Moore) and first printed in Madras, India, in 1970 as *The Arena*. It was subsequently published by the Holy Trinity Monastery, Jordanville, New York, in 1983.

These titles are currently available in the series *The Collected Works of St Ignatius (Brianchaninov)*:

Volume 1: The Field, Cultivating Salvation (Jordanville, New York: Holy Trinity Monastery, 2016) 978-0-88465-376-9

Volume 2: The Refuge, Anchoring the Soul in God (Jordanville, New York: Holy Trinity Monastery, 2019) 978-0-88465-429-2

Volume 5: The Arena, Guidelines for Spiritual and Monastic Life (Jordanville, New York: Holy Trinity Monastery, 2012) 978-0-88465-287-8

Notes

1. Letter 17, "To Hegumen Ilarion," *Letters to Monastics*, October 6, 1837.
2. Letter 19, "To Hegumen Varlam," *Letters to Monastics*, February 11, 1840.
3. Letter 26, "To Hegumen Bartholomew," *Letters to Monastics*, June 12, 1829.
4. Letter 29, "To Hegumen Bartholomew," *Letters to Monastics*, October 14, 1837.
5. Letter 36, "To Hegumen Bartholomew," *Letters to Monastics*, December 6, 1842.
6. Letter 63, "To Archimandrite Ignatius (Vasiliev)," *Letters to Monastics* [no date].
7. The reference here appears to be the French word for "pleasure," *plaisir*, which suggests doing something for empty pleasure, when there is nothing better to do.
8. Letter 65, *Letters to Monastics*, September 25 [no year given].
9. Letter 68, "To Archimandrite Ignatius (Vasiliev)," *Letters to Monastics*, October 23 [no year given].
10. Letter 72, "To Archimandrite Ignatius (Vasiliev)," *Letters to Monastics*, January 22 [no year given].
11. Probably an allusion to Matthew 10:30–31: "But the very hairs of your head are all numbered. 31 Do not fear therefore; you are of more value than many sparrows."
12. Letter 73, *Letters to Monastics*, March 20 [no year given].
13. Letter 74, "To Archimandrite Ignatius (Vasiliev)," *Letters to Monastics*, March 24, 1848.
14. From the Kontakion for the Departed sung at funerals and memorial services.
15. Letter 75, *Letters to Monastics*, 1847.
16. Letter 76, *Letters to Monastics* [no date].
17. Letter 77, *Letters to Monastics*, March 24, 1843.
18. *The Ladder of Divine Ascent* by St John Climacus.
19. Letter 79, *Letters to Monastics* [no date].
20. Possibly an allusion to Jeremiah 32:30: "Because the children of Israel and the children of Judah have done only evil before Me from their youth."
21. "God, be merciful to me a sinner!" Luke 18:13.
22. Letter 85, *Letters to Monastics*, October 9, 1842.
23. Letter 87, *Letters to Monastics* [no date].
24. Letter 88, *Letters to Monastics*, June 28, 1844.
25. Derived from Psalm 50:19.
26. Letter 91, *Letters to Monastics*, September 12, 1845.
27. From the service of monastic tonsure.
28. Letter 93, *Letters to Monastics*, May 20, 1846.
29. Letter 97, *Letters to Monastics*, April 2, 1858.
30. Letter 102, *Letters to Monastics* [no date].
31. Letter 107, *Letters to Monastics* [no date].
32. Letter 108, *Letters to Monastics* [no date].

33. Letter 109, *Letters to Monastics* [no date].
34. A monastic head covering.
35. Letter 110, *Letters to Monastics*, October 12 [no year given].
36. Letter 111, *Letters to Monastics* [no date].
37. See Matthew 8:14–15.
38. Letter 112, *Letters to Monastics* [no date].
39. Letter 113, *Letters to Monastics* [no date].
40. Descendants of a race of giants who inhabited part of the Promised Land. See Numbers 13.
41. A reference to the catapult used by David, when as a shepherd boy he defeated the giant Goliath. See 1 Sam 17.
42. Letter 114, *Letters to Monastics* [no date].
43. Letter 118, *Letters to Monastics*, October 9 [no year given].
44. Letter 120, *Letters to Monastics* [no date].
45. Letter 121, *Letters to Monastics* [no date].
46. Letter 122, *Letters to Monastics*, September 8, 1855.
47. Letter 123, *Letters to Monastics*, September 5, 1855.
48. Letter 125, *Letters to Monastics* [no date].
49. Letter 126, *Letters to Monastics*, October 9 [no year given].
50. An eleventh-century Byzantine ascetical writer.
51. The Biblical text referred to is "He who rejects Me, and does not receive My words, has that which judges him—the word that I have spoken will judge him in the last day (John 12:48).
52. A weed that was commonly found in nineteenth-century European wheatfields that is also beautiful.
53. Letter 127, *Letters to Monastics*, November 25, 1842.
54. Letter 133, *Letters to Monastics*, March 8, 1853.
55. Letter 149, *Letters to Monastics*, October 13, 1857.
56. 1 Tim 2:5: "For there is one God and one Mediator between God and men, the Man Christ Jesus."
57. Letter 155, *Letters to Monastics* [no date].
58. Letter 156, *Letters to Monastics*, September 5, 1847.
59. Descendants of Ham, the son of Noah, who inhabited the Promised Land (Canaan) prior to its conquest by the Israelites.
60. Letter 157, *Letters to Monastics*, October 12, 1847.
61. Letter 176, *Letters to Laity*, September 2, 1847.
62. Letter 177, *Letters to Laity*, September 4, 1847.
63. Letter 179, *Letters to Laity*, September 11, 1847.
64. Letter 180, *Letters to Laity* [no date].
65. Letter 181, *Letters to Laity* [no date].
66. Letter 182, *Letters to Laity*, September 24, 1847.
67. Letter 183, *Letters to Laity* [no date].
68. i.e., Satan
69. [Translator's note: St Ignatius seems to call the detailed analysis of sins a "dark cloak" worn by monastics who have experience with this kind of confession; this kind of confession is the product of a spiritually illumined mind, apparently, which

gives off inner light of sanctity in some ascetics. The "dark cloak" seems to be the virtual cloak the ascetic wears to hide his spiritual achievements from the world.]

70. Letter 184, *Letters to Laity* [no date].

71. Better known as "The False Dimitri." See https://en.wikipedia.org/wiki/False_Dmitry_I

72. St John Chrysostom.

73. [Translator's note: Cincinnatus is a Roman figure in the first century before Christ; his public service to Rome and to agriculture was legendary. In a time of great need, he gave up farming and raised an army for Rome and defeated the enemy.]

74. Letter 185, *Letters to Laity* [no date].

75. c. 1380–1471.

76. Letter 186, *Letters to Laity* [no date].

77. Letter 187, *Letters to Laity* [no date].

78. Letter 188, *Letters to Laity* [no date].

79. Letter 189, *Letters to Laity* [no date].

80. St Ignatius is probably alluding to Revelations 12:6: "Then the woman fled into the wilderness, where she has a place prepared by God." The woman is both Mary the Mother of God and a type of the Church.

81. Letter 190, *Letters to Laity* [no date].

82. Letter 191, *Letters to Laity* [no date].

83. [The Russian term is приходила . . .].

84. Letter 192, *Letters to Laity*, November 14, 1847.

85. Letter 193, *Letters to Laity* [no date].

86. Letter 194, *Letters to Laity*, December 27, 1847.

87. Letter 197, *Letters to Laity*, January 2, 1848.

88. The addressee of this letter seems to be a woman.

89. Letter 198, *Letters to Laity* [no date].

90. Letter 199, *Letters to Laity* [no date].

91. Letter 200, *Letters to Laity* [no date].

92. Letter 201, *Letters to Laity* [no date].

93. Letter 202, *Letters to Laity*, 1847.

94. Letter 203, *Letters to Laity* [no date].

95. Letter 204, *Letters to Laity*, February 4, 1848.

96. Letter 205, *Letters to Laity* [no date].

97. Letter 207, *Letters to Laity* [no date].

98. Letter 208, *Letters to Laity* [no date].

99. Letter 209, *Letters to Laity* [no date].

100. Letter 210, *Letters to Laity* [no date].

101. Letter 211, *Letters to Laity* [no date].

102. Letter 212, *Letters to Laity* [no date].

103. Letter 213, *Letters to Laity* [no date].

104. Letter 214, *Letters to Laity* [no date].

105. Letter 215, *Letters to Laity* [no date].

106. Letter 216, *Letters to Laity* [no date].

107. Letter 217, *Letters to Laity* [no date].

108. Letter 218, *Letters to Laity* [no date].

109. Both saints of the sixth century AD.

110. Bernard of Clairvaux, founder of the Cistercian monastic order in twelfth-century France.

111. Letter 219, *Letters to Laity* [no date].

112. Letter 220, *Letters to Laity* [no date].

113. Letter 221, *Letters to Laity* [no date].

114. Letter 222, *Letters to Laity* [no date].

115. Letter 223, *Letters to Laity* [no date].

116. Letter 224, *Letters to Laity* [no date].

117. Letter 225, *Letters to Laity* [no date].

118. Letter 226, *Letters to Laity* [no date].

119. Letter 227, *Letters to Laity* [no date].

120. From a traditional rite of Confession.

121. Letter 228, *Letters to Laity* [no date].

122. Letter 229, *Letters to Laity* [no date].

123. Letter 230, *Letters to Laity* [no date].

124. Letter 232, *Letters to Laity* [no date].

125. Letter 247, "To S.D. Nechaev," *Letters to Laity*, October 17, 1834 [Stefan Dimitrievich Nechaev (1792–1860)].

126. Letter 251, "To S.D. Nechaev," *Letters to Laity* [no date].

127. Letter 253, "To S.D. Nechaev," *Letters to Laity*, May 5, 1840.

128. Letter 256, "To S.D. Nechaev," *Letters to Laity*, April 11, 1841.

129. Letter 257, "To S.D. Nechaev," *Letters to Laity* [no date].

130. Letter 371, "To Maria Alexandrovna [St Ignatius' Sister]," *Letters to Family and Friends*, April 27, 1845.

131. Letter 381, "To Maria Alexandrovna," *Letters to Family and Friends*, April 27, 1845.

132. Letter 391, "To S.A.B-K-Noj [St Ignatius' Sister]," *Letters to Family and Friends* [no date].

133. Letter 395, "To Elizabeth Alexandrovna [St Ignatius' Sister] and Her Husband Dimitri Parensov," *Letters to Family and Friends*, April 13, 1847.

134. Letter 435, "To Elizabeth Alexandrovna," *Letters to Family and Friends*, March 14, 1862.

135. Letter 436, "To Elizabeth Alexandrovna," *Letters to Family and Friends*, December 21, 1863.

136. Letter 438, "To Elizabeth Alexandrovna," *Letters to Family and Friends*, June 28, 1864.

137. Letter 461, "To Peter Alexandrovich [St Ignatius' Brother]," *Letters to Family and Friends*, June 26, 1857.

138. Letter 469, "To Peter Alexandrovich," *Letters to Family and Friends*, September 4, 1861. [Letters 469 to 588 were written by St Ignatius when he served as Bishop of the Caucasus.]

139. Letter 508, "To Peter Alexandrovich," *Letters to Family and Friends*, January 4, 1864.

140. Letter 569, "To Monk Michael (Chikhachev)," *Letters to Family and Friends*, July 14, 1859.

141. Letter 577, "To Monk Michael (Chikhachev)," *Letters to Family and Friends*, May 25, 1860.

142. Letter 588, "To Monk Michael (Chikhachev)," *Letters to Family and Friends*, February 16, 1861.

Scripture Index

Note: In citations the letter "n" and a number refers to the note number on that page; for example p 183 (n.20) refers to the text associated with note 20 on page 183

Old Testament

Deuteronomy
    4:1, p. 65

Ecclesiastes
    1:18, p. 29

Exodus
    20:12, p. 60
    32:7–8, p. 64
    32:29, p. 70

Genesis
    1:26, p. 63
    3:5, p. 85
    3:19, p. 82
    37:35, p. 112
    48:22, p. 67

Isaiah
    21:4, p. 100
    53:5, p. 108
    64:5 LXX, p. 165

Jeremiah
    31:10 LXX, p. 72
    32:30, p. 183 (n.20)

Job
    1:21, p. 170

2 Kings
    11:25, p. 71

Numbers
    13, p. 184 (n.40)

13:32, p. 29
13:33, p. 29

Proverbs
    2:11, p. 150
    3:12, p. 175
    9:10, p. 99
    12:20 LXX, p. 98
    13:7, p. 54

Psalms
    5:19 LXX, p. 133
    6:2, p. 17
    17:30, 33 LXX, p. 73
    17:38–43, p. 29
    18:10 LXX, p. 144
    33:16, p. 24
    44:11, p. 17
    44:12, p. 17
    49:3 LXX, p. 136
    50:3, p. 14
    50:18–19, p. 137
    50:19, pp. 127, p. 183 (n.25)
    50:19 LXX, p. 145
    64:5, p. 103
    67:36, p. 92
    75:3, p. 58
    76:4, p. 127
    76:4 LXX, p. 169
    77:9, p. 30
    84:11, p. 27
    102:5, p. 83
    117:14, p. 17
    118:19, pp. 78, 127
    118:54, p. 81

HOLY TRINITY PUBLICATIONS
JORDANVILLE, NEW YORK

From the series:
The Collected Works of St Ignatius (Brianchaninov)

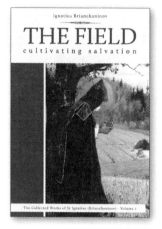

Volume I

The Field: Cultivating Salvation

The field is a place of cultivation and of battle. The author instructs his readers in the cultivation of the field of their hearts, with the aim of producing a harvest of virtues both pleasing to God and of benefit to all humankind. *The Field* draws deeply on the teachings of the ascetic fathers of the Church, from the desert dwellers of Scetis in Egypt to St Ignatius's Russian contemporaries, the Optina Elders.

ISBN: 9780884653769

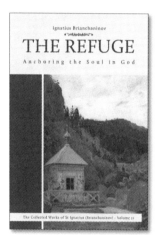

Volume II

The Refuge: Anchoring the Soul in God

Prayer is a refuge of God's great mercy to the human race. A refuge is a place of inner stillness and peace where the heart is fully opened to the embrace of God's love. This text is an exposition of the concrete actions one needs to take to live with and in God. It weaves together meditations on Scripture (from the Psalms in particular) and amplifies these with the wisdom of early Christian saints.

ISBN: 9780884654292

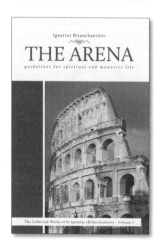

Volume V

The Arena: Guidelines for Spiritual and Monastic Life

This is one of the most important and accessible texts of Orthodox Christian teaching on the spiritual life, and not unlike the better known *Philokalia*. The author describes this work as his legacy "of soul saving instruction." In an age alienated from spiritual culture and rooted in materialism, his words pose an invitation to all who say to themselves "There must be more to life than this."

ISBN: 9780884652878